POOR SCHOLAR

POOR SCHOLAR

*A study of the works and days
of William Carleton (1794-1869)*

by

BENEDICT KIELY

THE TALBOT PRESS
89 TALBOT STREET
DUBLIN 1

DEDICATED
TO
MY PARENTS

FIRST EDITION 1947
THIS EDITION 1972

SET IN 10 ON 11PT TIMES ROMAN
SBN 85452 017 1

PRINTED IN THE REPUBLIC OF IRELAND FOR
THE TALBOT PRESS LTD.
89 TALBOT STREET DUBLIN 1

FOREWORD

THIS STUDY of William Carleton, the greatest novelist that Ireland in the nineteenth century gave to the English language, does not attempt to follow in chronological detail the story of his life. His own unfinished autobiography, and the patient pages in which O'Donoghue mentioned the notable things in the years left uncovered by the autobiography, have done that work of narrative better than any writer nowadays could hope to do it. But Carleton had in relation to the Ireland of his time a significance not shared by his contemporaries, by Lever or Gerald Griffin or the Banims or Mrs. Hall. His life and his writing bridged the Famine, the greatest of the many tragedies of the Irish nineteenth century. His own character mirrored much of the contradiction and division, political and religious, of that period, just as the journey that brought him from his birthplace in Tyrone to the place where his body was laid in Dublin emphasises the continuance of some of those divisions and contradictions into the present.

In an attempt to outline the man's significance this book has been written. The material used will be found mostly in his own works, not widely read nowadays, not even always easily available. After his own works comes the tireless, not always accurate, digging of O'Donoghue; and then the novels and comments of contemporary writers. As a general rule any debt is acknowledged immediately in a footnote. It remains only to thank those friends who have for my benefit resurrected and loaned to me scarce editions of some of Carleton's books.

The chronology that follows indicates the dates of the first publication—sometimes in serial form and sometimes in book form—of his more important works. It is based, obviously enough, on the fairly exhaustive list given by O'Donoghue. For the reader's guidance a few other notable dates of the period have been introduced.

CHRONOLOGY

1794   William Carleton born at Prillisk, near Clogher, County Tyrone.

1798   The year of the rebellion.
Birth of John Banim in Kilkenny.

1803   Birth of Gerald Griffin in Limerick.

1806   Birth of Charles Lever in Dublin.

1811   Maria Edgeworth acknowledges the authorship of *Castle Rackrent*.

1814   Thomas Davis born in Mallow, County Cork.

1816   Charles Gavan Duffy born in Monaghan.

1818   Carleton arrives in Dublin.

1820   His marriage with Jane Anderson.

1827   His meeting with Caesar Otway.

1828   Publication in the *Christian Examiner* of 'The Lough Derg Pilgrim' and 'Father Butler.' In the same year Griffin's novel *The Collegians* appeared.

1830   First series of the *Traits and Stories of the Irish Peasantry* published in two volumes.

1831   'Denis O'Shaughnessy Going to Maynooth,' published in the *Christian Examiner*.

1833   'Neal Malone' published in *Dublin University Review and Quarterly*; 'The Dead Boxer' in *Dublin University Magazine*; and the second series of the *Traits and Stories* in three volumes.

1834   *Tales of Ireland* (one volume).

1836   *Jane Sinclair* or *The Fawn of Springvale*.
In that year he went with Samuel Ferguson on a walking tour in North Wales.

1837   A German translation of the *Traits and Stories* published at Leipzig. 'Fardorougha the Miser, or The Convicts of Lisnamona' appeared as a serial in the *Dublin University Magazine*; and in the following year was published in one volume.

1840   *Irish Penny Journal* founded. It published many of Carleton's lighter character studies: 'The Irish Fiddler,' 'The Country Dancing-master,' 'Rose Moan, the Irish Midwife,' etc.

1842   The *Traits and Stories* published in numbers with illustrations by Phiz, Wrightson, Gibson, Lee, Franklin, MacManus, Harvey, and Gilbert. Afterwards published in two volumes (London and Dublin).

In the same year John Banim died. Lever took over the editorship of the *Dublin University Magazine*. Davis, Dillon and Gavan Duffy planned the prospectus for the *Nation*.

1845 First publication of *Valentine McClutchy, the Irish Agent*, or *Chronicles of the Castle Cumber Property* (three volumes, Dublin, with plates by Phiz). *Rody the Rover*, or *The Ribbonman* (one volume). *Parra Sastha*, or *The History of Paddy-Go-Easy and his Wife Nancy* (one volume). *Tales and Stories of the Irish Peasantry* (one volume with illustrations by Phiz). *Les Chroniques de Chateau Cumber* commenced as a serial in *L'Univers*. *Art Maguire*, or *The Broken Pledge* (one volume: Dublin).

In the same year Thomas Davis died.

1846 *The Black Prophet* made its first appearance in the *Dublin University Magazine*.

He revisited his native place in the Clogher Valley.

1847 The worst year of famine. In that year he met Thomas Carlyle.

The Emigrants of Ahadarra (one volume: Belfast and London).

1849 *The Tithe Proctor* (one volume: Belfast).

In that year Maria Edgeworth died.

1850 *The Clarionet, The Dead Boxer*, and *Barney Branagan* (one volume: Dublin). *Willy Reilly and his dear Cooleen Bawn* first appeared in the *Independent Newspaper*, London. In the same year Carleton visited London.

1851 *The Squanders of Castle Squander* first appeared in the *Illustrated London News*.

1852 *Red Hall*, or *The Baronet's Daughter* (three volumes: London). *The Squanders of Castle Squander* (two volumes: London).

1855 *Willy Reilly and his dear Cooleen Bawn* (three volumes: London).

1857 *The Black Baronet*, or *Chronicles of Ballytrain*. This was a revision of *Red Hall*, the change of title being the result of Carleton's quarrel with the publisher, McGlashan. *Alley Sheridan*, or *The Runaway Marriage, and other stories* (reprinted from the *National Magazine*).

1860 *The Evil Eye*, or *The Black Spectre* (one volume: Dublin).

1861 *The Double Prophecy* or *Trials of the Heart* serialised in Duffy's *Hibernian Magazine*. *Romans Irlandais*: three tales from the *Traits and Stories* translated into French by L. De Wailly (one volume: Paris).

1862 *Redmond Count O'Hanlon, the Irish Rapparee*, reprinted from Duffy's *Hibernian Magazine* (one volume: Dublin). *The Silver Acre, and other tales* (one volume: London). *The*

      Double Prophecy, or *Trials of the Heart* (two volumes: Dublin).

1864   *Traits and Stories*, fifth complete illustrated edition (two volumes: London).

1865   *L'oeil mauvais, ou le spectre noir* (one volume: Paris).

1869   Death of Carleton.

1870   *The Red-Haired Man's Wife*, published in the *Carlow College Magazine*. *The Fair of Emyvale*: *The Master and the Scholar* (one volume: London).

1876   *Traits and Stories*, eleventh complete edition (one volume: London).

1878   *Willy Reilly and his dear Cooleen Bawn*, fortieth edition (one volume: Dublin).

1881   Another edition of the *Traits and Stories*.

1882   *The Works of William Carleton* (Collier: New York).

1889   *The Red-Haired Man's Wife* (one volume: Dublin).

1896   *The Life of William Carleton*: Being his autobiography and letters; and an account of his life and writings, from the point at which the autobiography breaks off, by David J. O'Donoghue. With an introduction by Mrs. Cashel Hoey. In two volumes with two portraits (Downey: London).

CONTENTS

PROLOGUE

IT IS not mountainy land. It is not flat land. The tarred roads, linking the little towns together, rise and fall regularly over round rich hills, farmed to the top, held in place by a network of deep whispering hedges. Here and there the primitive force of the earth revolts from rich greenery, from fruitful furrows drawn by the rigid coulter; rises up into sombre moorland, or a ridge covered with coarse heather, or a hill planted with straight trees. The roads rise and fall, dropping into little glens where the leaves and the roadside grasses are unbelievably quiet, going over round hills to open up visions of infinite blue distances, with mountains very low and far away on an uncertain horizon. Under a sultry sky on a warm July day the place has something symbolic of everything in the genius of the man that the place made: richness and colour in the good, farmed land; in the moors and the occasional rocks something unkempt and desolate and always out of control; in those blue, infinite spaces some suggestion of greatness and power, never exactly defined, never stabilised and made permanent.

A line from Omagh on the Strule, which is another name for the upper waters of the Foyle, to Enniskillen on the Erne, would mark approximately the western boundary of that land. On the south it could be enclosed by a line linking Enniskillen with Clones, with Monaghan, with Saint Patrick's Armagh; always remembering that the Monaghan country opens naturally out to the sea at Dundalk; that between Monaghan and Newry is a mountainous country with its own peculiar characteristics and its own influence in the making of any man from South Tyrone or North Monaghan. Then from Armagh the eastern boundary returns to Omagh by way of Dungannon, a town on a great hill where Hugh O'Neill defied Elizabeth, where Grattan's Volunteers came in the eighteenth century to a colourful Convention. Further to the east is the flat expanse of Lough Neagh; while north of Omagh there is the cartwheel of mountain ridges centring at Mullagharn, and beyond Mullagharn the Sperrins.

Inside the area defined by those lines is the Clogher Valley of South Tyrone with the little musically-named towns of Ballygawley, Aughnacloy, Augher, Clogher and Fivemiletown. Knockmany Hill is visible from the vicinity of each one of the five; and remembering the loveliness of that valley he wrote a poem about Knockmany, not an exceptionally good poem, but a poem filled with that passionate attachment to the environment of childhood that was one of the best parts of the man. Between Clogher and

3

Knockmany is the townland of Prillisk, high hedges and rich green fields, where William Carleton was born in 1794.

Beginning in those fields you can go back to follow the ways of a boy, to find the soul of a boy. It is an uneasy journey. The years cut across it, with a dozen changes, a dozen revolutions, with one black visitation of hunger that may have been an act of God or the work of man's wickedness, but was, anyway, a sour and withering desolation. But it is not so much the years. The way back is confused by voices: voices from the past praising him and damning him, voices of men and women who knew him, the less assured voices of those who lived since and knew him only by hearsay or through the stories he told, the voices of his own people in the present talking confusedly about a hundred things.

They say: 'He knew us in the cabins. But we are not in the cabins any more. We don't read his books any more. Printers don't print them any more. Even when we did read his books we never knew whether to be pleased or angry or terribly ashamed.'

He knew them in the cabins. He came with them out of the cabins, in a time of hunger and unease and miserable change, in a time of chaos more than a century since, when even the strongest weren't sure of their footing. He was never one of the strongest, never one of the most stable. But he had imagination, rich humour, a capacity for honourable tears. He went with them to weddings and wakes, funerals, christenings, places of prayer, places of merriment. He knew them when they were many, when—in spite of much misery—they were reasonably erect upon the earth. He saw that black, withering visitation of famine. All these things he remembered and wrote down; and, for their sake, he wrote two or three of the world's great stories.

He had his credit for it; not much money, for he was a bad man at business; not much worldly comfort, beyond the fragrance of poteen punch, or the beauty of rivers and mountains and green fields, or the love and contentment around his own hearth. But he had praise from great men who were few, from small men who were many, and from some he had blame and bitter words.

He knew the Ireland of the cabins, he came from the cabins; and Charles Gavan Duffy, who had travelled a somewhat similar road, saw Carleton rising like a mountain above the men of his time. The particular mountain mentioned was Slieve Donard, the highest mountain in the province of Ulster in which both Carleton and Duffy were born.

Thomas Davis was one of the best men that Carleton spoke with as a friend, and Davis, reading Carleton's stories, saw 'the moory upland and the corn slopes, the glen where the rock juts through mantling heather and bright brooks gurgle amid the scented banks

4

of wild herbs, the shivering cabin and the rudely-lighted farm-house.' For Davis all these things were as plain as if Carleton had used canvas and colours, as Wilson did, or Poussi or Teniers or Wilkie.

Caryle from Chelsea, growling his way through Ireland, influencing and annoying John Mitchel, still convinced in his Scottish soul that Oliver Cromwell had been Ireland's greatest friend, saw Carleton as a 'genuine bit' of the old Ireland that Cromwell had befriended.

Dr. Murry of Maynooth College wrote about him in the *Edinburgh Review* and, in spite of much that a Maynooth man might have taken offence at, found him not only Irish but 'thoroughly Irish, intensely Irish, exclusively Irish.' Future times would turn to his pages, and only to his pages, for the clearest picture of men and their manners in Ireland before and during that withering visitation, men who before long would 'have passed away from that troubled land, from the records of history, and from the memory of man for ever.'

T. P. O'Connor, a politician, a journalist, and a character, saw him as a man who had 'enriched the literary world for ever with unsurpassed pathos—with a laughter as spontaneous and as human as that of Cervantes.' He saw him as a man who had given the world a truer key to the heart of Ireland than any writer who had ever lived.

Lady Wilde, a poetess and the mother of a very unfortunate poet, consoled him in his half-real, half-imagined misery, put something of what she thought about him into verse:

He struck the keynote of a people's heart
And all the nation answered to his touch.

Yeats, the poet, heard a great deal about him from Lady Wilde, called him 'our greatest humorist', noticed how near his laughter was to tears. The history of a nation was, said Yeats, 'not in parliaments and battlefields, but in what the people say to each other on fair-days and high days, and in how they farm and quarrel and go on pilgrimage.' Carleton had done Ireland, and the people of Ireland for ever, the great service of recording these things. He was 'the great novelist of Ireland by right of the most Celtic eyes that ever gazed from under the brow of story-teller.' The poet, somewhere between the Celtic twilight and the Indian twilight and the twilight of the nineteenth century, found in Carleton's longer novels 'a clay-cold melancholy' that made their author kin with the animals in Milton's puritan Paradise 'half-emerged only from the earth and its brooding.'

5

An academic American[1] thought that Carleton as a novelist of the manners of the peasantry had beaten out all English and Scottish competitors in the same field.

Sir Shane Leslie looking back from our own days compares[2] him with every man or woman who has attempted to dip a pen in 'Irish gall or gaiety', and always the comparison is in Carleton's favour. The 'finished artistry' of the remarkable Miss Edgeworth, who had inspired Scott and Turgenev and been dictated to by her remarkable, much-married father, paled before the 'rich torrential canvas' that was Carleton. 'Lever dissipated himself for a perrennial after-dinner audience. Lover was Lever running to seed. Lady Morgan was an ambitious Miss Edgeworth. Mrs. Hall wrote for a Baedeker unborn.' Carleton himself said that the good Mrs. Hall never could have known the people of Ireland as well as he knew them, for she had never been drunk in their company. She certainly hadn't. But Carleton had been drunk in their company and sober in their company, had praised Father Mathew and total abstinence for their edification, had praised poteen punch because it was worthy of praise, had spoken English to them and Irish to them. He 'caught his types', writes Shane Leslie, 'before Ireland made the greatest plunge in her history and the famine had cleaned her to the bone. For the hardiest of the race rose up and went away into the West, of which their story-tellers had been telling them for a thousand years.'

One hundred years ago the people of this small Atlantic island made a fearful plunge into misery, died and rotted in thousands, sailed westwards in thousands, very literally 'pursuing the ghost of Brendan's mast.' In the west they survived, built themselves into the body of something very different from the fragrant isles that delighted medieval legends. Incredibly, those who stayed at home, the remnant of a people, also survived, stubbornly fighting their way back to solid ground where the present would have stability and freedom and a clear meaning, where even the horror of the past would have its own sanative and instructive value. The man, who had been a boy in Prillisk in Tyrone, found or was allotted a place among the lessons that the past was to teach. We did not learn those lessons with patience, or from plain writing on a blackboard, or from deliberate pedagogic dictation, but hurriedly, and influenced always by our own caprice and self-will. We did not particularly like the lesson implicit in this man who had in him also so much caprice, so much self-willed, unrestrained imagination. For he saw us in our deepest degradation like men caught naked in

[1] Horatio Sheafe Krans in *Irish Life in Irish Fiction* (Columbia University Press New York, 1903)

[2] In a preface to Rose Shaw's *Carleton's Country* (Talbot Press, Dublin)

6

a cold street in the white light of day. He gave offence, wrote his more-or-less official biographer,[1] 'to every class of Irishman in one or other of his books, and all that can be done by way of extenuation or excuse is to explain the incidents which seem to have occasioned his conduct.'

I do not know if they can even be explained as simply as all that. For the mystery of the man's soul, or of the soul of any man, is hidden from us as completely as the awful secret behind that century-old suffering, the awful secret behind all suffering. In his own chaotic and entangled soul he has mirrored all our own complication, has hinted at the chaos into which we plunged, almost to perish, but ultimately to survive.

I only know that, in the one place in the world where he found men and women and made them immortal, the meaning behind the mystery, the secret lost somewhere in chaos, do not seem to be of any account. Sheltering in a cottage doorway from a sudden shower, or talking with men thinning turnips on a hill in Prillisk, or going up steeply through new-planted trees to the top of Knockmany Hill, the present is the past, the people are unchanged, the black cloth of famine might never have swept across the century. In the one-sided town of Clogher a saddler says proudly that he lives in the house in Springtown where Carleton once lived. It must be remembered that this was written in the 1940s. In the 1970s the saddler's widow still proudly lives in that house which has been inhabited since the 18th century. Her people have lived there since Carleton's father died. In the hazel glen behind that house the blackbirds sing eternally, as he heard them through the open window singing their souls to the rich cool evening. Across the road from the Forth chapel the girl in the shop talks about the Yankee soldiers who camped near Aughentain. The stories he, in his time, heard and wrote down were about Cromwellian soldiers laying siege to the castle of Aughentain, about Rose the miller's daughter in the mill of Aughentain. But there is justice in that change; for, although for the sake of a happy ending to the novel to which they gave a name, the emigrants of Ahadarra really stayed at home, the other Irish townlands were not so fortunate. And if the sons and grandsons of the exiles return, wearing the uniform of the great Western republic, it is only the justice of God on Cromwellianism in the past and Cromwellianism in all places and at all times.

Leaning over the wall beside the shop the saddler from Clogher points to Dunroe or to Richardson's house where the hedge-school

---

[1] *The Life of William Carleton.* Being his autobiography and letters; and an account of his life and writings, from the point at which the Autobiography breaks off. By David J. O'Donoghue. With an introduction by Mrs. Cashel Hoey (2 vols. Downey London, 1896).

was. And it is easy to see Carleton, more than a century since, walking these narrow roads, learning a little about books, learning a lot about men and women, his own immortal, imperishable people—leaving us a lot to learn from the story of his days.

In the house at Springtown there is a radio set, made by a Canadian visitor for the saddler's daughter. Over it the voice of the world comes to the quiet valley, mingling with the song of the blackbird in the hazel glen, with the confused contradictory voices of the past century. But if you listen carefully you will hear the one voice that matters most of all, speaking across a hundred years, speaking for the people of this valley, for the people of Ireland, for those who died, and those who live, for those who sailed over the sea, even for those who returned to camp where the soldiers of Cromwell once camped in the townland of Aughentain.

ONE

IN DISTANT Dublin a high governmental official said that when he was finished with the people they would be as tame as cats. For the time, which was about 1798, and the place, Ireland, it was a typical interpretation of the duties of those in power to those who suffered government. So soldiers with arms and authority and utterly without discipline, and sectarian societies burning and murdering by night, did their best to fulfil the purposes of high government, to reduce the people to felinity. Not glossy, smooth, well-fed, contented domesticated cats, but animals wickedly ready to strike back and destroy.

The sight of soldiers very naturally struck terror into the people. Young or old, men or women were equally liable to assault, torture, mutilation or murder. A man of seventy seeing a party of soldiers fled instinctively. They followed him. He knelt, begging for mercy. One soldier, testing his own ability, beheaded him where he knelt, with only one blow. An old man in the dusk, mending his cart outside his own door, was hacked to pieces by a gallant captain because he had violated an act of government telling him to be indoors after sunset. A boy, who held open a gate for two mounted soldiers riding through, was shot dead for no particular reason, and cut up with precision and deliberation. Tom the Devil, who was a sergeant in the North Cork Militia, invented the linen cap bubbling with boiling pitch, and added a lot to the fun for himself and his friends-in-arms. A woman wearing a green dress or even a green ribbon was really asking for criminal assault, but then no woman was safe in any colour of dress or ribbon. In Drogheda town a solid citizen was flogged to death for wearing a ring with a shamrock device; a young man, suspected of knowing where arms were concealed, cut his throat rather than endure the final instalment of the 5,000 lashes to which he had been sentenced. In Dublin the streets were remarkably quiet and empty of people; those who could, left hurriedly for England; prisoners were taken until the jails were full to the doors; droves of men went to compulsory service in the fleet; men screamed under flogging at Beresford's Riding School; a young fellow with a burning pitch-cap on his head ran shrieking down the quays, leaping for cool death into the Liffey water; the giant Lieutenant Hepenstall walked, like something in a Dantesque vision, strangling men over his monstrous shoulders.

In Bantry Bay was the frustrated flapping of French sails; along a road in Connaught the belated and utterly futile 'dance of the French drums.'

9

A staunch Scottish general called Abercromby who could not see his way to reducing men and women to the level of cats, wild or domesticated, compared the crimes of the King's soldiers to the crimes of Cossacks and Calmucks, said that, in the event of real fighting, the soldiers would be formidable to everyone but the enemy, eventually threw up his command in disgust and returned to England. Fighting did begin. First of all there were arrests in Dublin, young men with French principles, not really part of the persecuted people but feeling for them a classical, visionary feeling. Napoleon Bonaparte, foolishly dazzled by the East, sailed from Toulon with 20,000 valuable men. On the same day in Dublin Lord Edward Fitzgerald was taken by Major Sirr, Major Sandyes and Captain Ryan. Then within a week trouble began and ended in the eastern midlands; General Dundas tramped on the trouble-makers and high government sat back to congratulate itself on the end of the rebellion. The soldiers surpassed the Cossacks and Calmucks, flogging and applying the pitch-cap, rubbing moistened gun-powder into the hair of victims and then setting the hair burning; until finally in Wexford county, where high government had least expected it, the incredible patience of the people broke in fighting and blood and burning buildings. The end, inevitably, was defeat.

Closer to the Clogher valley the few exceptional Presbyterian rebels, inspired by revolutionary France, attacked the town of Antrim, captured Saintfield and Newtownards, were beaten by General Nugent at Ballinahinch. That was as near as the fighting came to Prillisk, apart from those bitter, sectarian raidings and burnings that set neighbour against neighbour, hardened the little homes of Ulster with a hate that belonged to Calvin's sour Geneva. Not twenty miles away in Omagh town six thousand Presbyterians, alarmed by a few truths and fifty lies about Catholic outrages, volunteered to serve against the Wexford rebels.

Then one night in mid-winter there was a battering at the door of his father's house, much bellowing of uncomplimentary remarks about traitors and rebels. The yeomen crowded in over the threshold, armed and uniformed, bayonets screwed on their guns and pointed menacingly at his father who, shivering in his underclothes, held up a single candle against the black night and the wintry wind puffing in spasmodically at the open door. They wanted the old man's gun, the papist gun, the rascal rebelly gun. They called his father a liar. They called his mother a liar. They jabbed his sister in the side with a bayonet because the bed in which she lay might conceal a gun; and, when she screamed with pain, one yeoman, more humane than the others, called the man who used the bayonet a cowardly scoundrel. In the end they discovered that the cause of the trouble was a toy gun given to the Carleton children by Sam Nelson, a neighbouring Protestant, a good-natured slob of a man. Sam's brother was one of the raiding yeomen.

He remembered that incident against the yeomen. He remembered it against Orangeism, against bigotry, against the glorious, pious and immortal memory of the Dutch king who crossed the Boyne on a white horse. He remembered it when he wrote the great, violent book about Valentine McClutchy, the Irish agent, and Solomon McSlime, the religious and adulterous attorney. He was only a boy. He was born into an unfortunate country at a terrible chaotic time, and on that wintry night he had come up against one of the things that made the country unfortunate: bigotry, bitterness, the neighbour crossing your threshold in his yeoman's uniform, with his gun and prodding bayonet.

Con the Convulsionist,[1] at the great council of vagabonds and beggars praised himself as the man who simulated convulsions better than any other man living 'barring Bet, my wife, who bates me in frothing at the mouth.' With this qualification Con recommended himself to his fellow-scamps as a worthy aspirant to a seat in the Irish Parliamentary Party, as the most natural of Irishmen because Ireland was always in a convulsion of some kind or other.

Carleton's first experience of Ireland's chronic convulsions was that one night-raid echoing faintly the fighting, the blood, the bigotry, the flogging and torture. Looking back on it afterwards he wrote: 'Merciful God! In what a frightful condition was the country at that time. I speak now of the North of Ireland. It was then, indeed, the seat of Orange ascendancy and irresponsible power. To find a justice of the peace *not* an Orangeman would have been an impossibility. The grand jury room was little less than an Orange lodge. There was then no law *against* an Orangeman, and no law *for* a Papist.'[2]

From convulsion to convulsion, all his life long. Towards the end he put on the lips of Father Moran[3] these solemn words of foreboding: 'There is a black cloud at this moment about to overshadow the land . . . it will cover us as with a thick garment, and horror, dismay and death will be written in every face; a storm will arise, blood will be shed, men will be tortured and slain for loving the faith of their fathers, and where coercion fails, gold will be tried.'

That same note of desolation could have been sounded in Ireland during all the years of his life. Convulsion after convulsion, desolation following desolation. No law that favoured a Papist. No law that favoured the poor. He was born into chaos.

1 *The Squanders of Castle Squander.*
2 O'Donoghue's *Life of Carleton*, vol. i, p. 29.
3 *The Red-Haired Man's Wife*, p. 104.

11

From rebellion, night-raiding, sporadic fighting and continuous and consistent atrocity the transition to dancing and devilment is made simply enough through the person of Buckramback the country dancing-master. Little Buckramback, with his mixture of Tipperary and illegitimate English on his tongue, with a back cartilaginous from frequent flogging, danced into Carleton's country, into Carleton's life, into Irish literature. Sometimes, somewhere in the British army he had beaten the drum, learned to play the fiddle, endured the floggings that gave him his name and his amazing fortitude when, as a '98 rebel, he took what '98 rebels got when they were lucky, and afterwards danced a jig before Lord Cornwallis. Young Carleton was more interested in his dancing feet, in everything symbolised by dancing, than in the national calamity of which Buckramback's impervious skin was one minute part. In a barn at Kilnahushogue the little fellow, in his crimped, black, secondhand coat, tiny pumps, tiny white stockings, coaxed, drab breeches, taught the country-boys and girls how to enter a drawing-room 'in the most fashionable manner alive.' The gentlemen learned how to 'shiloote' the ladies. The ladies and gentlemen learned how to bow and 'curchy,' learned the art of courtship as—according to Buckramback—it was practised with all politeness and success in Paris, learned how to write love-letters and valentines as—again the Gallic touch—Bonaparte had written them to both his wives.

But the real business was the dance, no rude leaping and bounding, but quadrilles, waltzes, the dances of fashion, the Sir Roger de Coverley or Helter-Skelter Drag 'in which every gentleman was at liberty to pull every leedy where he plaised, and every leedy was at liberty to go wherever he pulled her.'

There was high courtesy in that barn, the savour of fashion, the noble gesture of chivalry and a link with gallant France, all touched a little with pathos and tinged with delicious irony. The reality was robustious fun, exquisite idleness, summing-up and symbolising all the valuable garnering idleness of his years in the valley. Buckramback could ask Paddy Corcoran to step out now and enter his drawing-room as a gentleman should, or he could enquire of Grauna Mulholland whether or not she knew her five positions and her fifteen attitudes. But in barns and cottages all over Ireland a thousand Paddies and Graunas were raising the dust and shaking the floor, or courting on the seats around the wall, on sacks of corn laid lengthwise, or logs of round timber, or upturned creels or iron pots. The young girls wore white; their solid bachelors rejoiced in broadcloth coats, yellow buff vests, corduroy small-clothes. Circled by the wise and the elderly, the blind fiddler set the pace for a movement and merriment that defied poverty and laughed in the face of hunger. Carleton was part of it, pirouetting at the pleasure of Buckramback, or moving unrestrainedly with the whole dancing people, enjoying himself, being delightfully idle.

Years later he sat down to meditate and reflect. This is what he wrote: 'The Irish dance, like every other assembly composed of Irishmen and Irishwomen, presents the spectator with those traits which enter into our conception of rollicking fun and broad humour. The very arrangements are laughable; and when joined to the eccentric strains of some blind fiddler like Barney Dhal, to the grotesque and caricaturish faces of the men, and the modest, but evidently arch and laughter-loving countenances of the females, they cannot fail to impress an observing mind with the obvious truth that a nation so thoughtless and easily directed from the serious and useful pursuits of life to such scenes, can seldom be industrious and wealthy, nor, despite their mirth and humour, a happy people.'[1]

But back in the barn in the valley he was not a spectator. He was unconsciously observing and assimilating, but he was not an 'observing mind.' He was Billy Carleton, dancing with the best of them, big and active and strong and handsome and a boyo with the girls. He was shouting with the crowd at Paddy and Katty dancing on a board, marvelling at the suppleness of Paddy who would almost dance *The Dusty Miller* on a floor paved with drawn razors. He was the soul incarnate of the brag-dancers up on the table to display to the fluid chant of the bag-pipes their exceptional, individual powers. He was idle. He was learning in idleness. He had not met Caesar Otway. And in spite of later moralisings he was lustily and outrageously happy.

The noisy dancers could be attentively quiet around the hearth listening to the man with stories to tell or the woman with music and a sweet, singing voice and melodious songs to sing. Stories of Goll who might, according to the proverb, be found some day wrestling with God on the Fenian meadows, or songs of love and sorrow and lost causes, were much closer to reality than poor Buckramback's efforts to introduce Paddy and Grauna to a completely hypothetical drawing-room. A child in the corner, warm with ashes, or rocked in his wooden cradle, he could have looked up when the house filled with neighbours in the evening, heard his father tell such stories, heard his mother sing such songs. His father was a pious man, able to repeat nearly the whole of the Old and New Testaments by heart. His father was an industrious man. Going and coming over the little green hills around Prillisk, helping the neighbours with their flax, his mind was all the time as active as his skilled hands. All his life he had been hearing stories and remembering

[1] 'The Midnight Mass' (*Traits and Stories of the Irish Peasantry*).

13

them, expanding and elaborating them, gathering a treasury of coloured things to tell around his own hearth, passing them on to a son who was to tell stories in a different way and even in a different language. Always, running like a river of gold under the stories of the things the son had actually seen, was the richness that had passed to him from the lips of his labouring, praying, story-telling father. The richness now and again came up like a fountain or a spring coloured by the sun. There was the tale of the traditional three tasks imposed on Jack MacGennis of the Routing Burn when he was foolish enough to play cards with a black man and a talking dog that smoked a pipe as sober as a judge.[1] There was the ballad about the weird spirit in the churchyard of Erigle Truagh who appeared as a man to women, as a woman to men, and kissed them into death by way of 'pleuritic fever.' There was the proud boast that neither Petrie, Betham, Ferguson, O'Donovan or any other antiquary or folklorist had anything to teach to the man whose childhood had been spent in the Clogher Valley listening to his father's stories and his mother's songs.

She sang as Irish women had sung for centuries before: with a voice rounded and sweet almost beyond human sweetness, a voice with trills and melodious grace-notes, the body rocking gently to and fro. The language in which she sang was going down to something very close to total extinction but, even if her son was a peasant bred in poverty he was no politician and, unlike Daniel O'Connell, his great Kerry contemporary, he was never prepared to despise a beautiful thing because it had ceased to be useful. The songs his mother sang were beautiful. The language in which those songs were written was, by association, beautiful. All through his life the echoes of that voice, the melody of the words were alive in his soul. He remembered the day when she had grudgingly consented to sing an English version of a song that afterwards gave him the name of a book: *The Red-Haired Man's Wife*. She said the English words and the air were like a man and his wife quarrelling. She said the Irish melted into the music, the English didn't.

In moments of strong passion or deep sorrow the people of his stories turn instinctively to the language in which his mother preferred to sing. In her deepest misery and sorrow the wife of Art Maguire the drunkard crooned over her sleeping child a Gaelic lullaby, 'a tender but melancholy air.'[2] Over the dead body of the boy Torley O'Regan his parents spoke softly in their own language and gave to their dialogue a 'figurative style and tenderness of expression.'[3] And later in the story the distracted woman mourning both her husband and her child 'began to sing an old and

---

[1] *Traits and Stories.*   [2] *Art Maguire*, p. 119.
[3] *Valentine McClutchy.*

14

melancholy Irish air, in a voice whose sweetness was in singular keeping with its mournful spirit.' When the strange, wild woman walked one day into the house of Mrs. Sullivan, the good woman, crushing down terror and repulsion, welcomed and blessed her 'in those kindly phrases so peculiar to the Irish language.'[1] And Jemmy McEvoy, the poor scholar, returning, an ordained priest, to his people, ran to his mother saying: 'I will speak to her in Irish. It will go directly to her heart.'[2]

He could not very easily escape the Irish language. It was still the native language of a very large section of the people, spoken, wrote Thomas Davis, by 'half the people west of a line drawn from Derry to Waterford.' It found its way into the novels of Charles Lever, where, in *Luttrell of Aran*, old Malone prays in Irish, where Kate O'Hara talks in her delirium in Irish, and where Sir Within, the old man of the world, sacks the maid called Molly because Molly had spoken Irish to Miss O'Hara and reminded her of her peasant origins. Gerald Griffin, with a slight touch of the language revivalist of a later time, could be caustic about the clerk who thought it genteel not to know Irish.[3] Carleton could be less obviously and more humorously caustic about the determination of the valiant Hycy Burke,[4] trying hard to be a gentleman, resolved not to speak the language that ke knew better than English.

For the whole movement of the world, since the world had its centre in London, was set steady against the survival of the language spoken for centuries on the island of Ireland. The boy in the valley found the words on the tongues of the people in a state of unsettlement and disorder. Philologically, even, they swung in emptiness. With the art of a great humorist, born to squeeze fun out of every-thing, he could make merry at the bewilderment of his people in a world where even words kept contradicting each other. Tom Gressiey, shoemaker by trade and story-teller by blood, tradition and aptitude, was, when he recited in Gaelic, as completely at home as blind Homer declaiming in Greek. But Tom speaking English was an incredibly comic person who had by heart the phraseology of Pastorini's prophecies, the *Seven Champions of Christendom*, *Think Well On't*, and Donlevy's catechism. Even the very interchange of affection and the work of Mary Murray the match-maker needed at times the aid of an interpreter. He had seen weddings with one party speaking English, the other speaking Irish, only with difficulty understanding each other. When, in debate,[5] the minister

---

1 'The Lianhan Shee' (*Traits and Stories*).
2 'The Poor Scholar' (*Traits and Stories*).
3 *The Collegians*.
4 *Emigrants of Ahadarra*.
5 *Squanders of Castle Squander*

15

Dr. McClaret staggered Randy O'Rollick with a mathematical conundrum Randy's retort was to ask him in Irish what was the latest news from Purgatory and whether his father's soul was yet redeemed out of it. The doctor, who had once been a Catholic, was beaten, not by the fact that professionally he didn't believe in Purgatory but because he couldn't speak Irish; and Randy explained triumphantly that he had spoken in 'the vernacular of a certain country with whose history you are evidently unacquainted, of a country whose inhabitants live upon a meal a month, keep very little—for sound reasons—between themselves and the elements, and where abstinence from food is the national diversion.' Paddy Dimnick,[1] the voteen, who said his prayers in the branches of a tree, spoke of the son of the Virgin Mary who suffered on a tree; and a footnote commented: 'This is a usual epithet given in the Irish language to Christ by Romanists.'

For Caesar Otway, the lean proselytiser, had never heard the voice of Mary Kelly the mother of William Carleton singing by the hearth songs of love and sorrow and imperishable beauty. Even Mary Kelly's son, born of a bewildered people in a time of contradiction, knew moments when that voice was no longer heard as he heard it, maybe, going out of the house to sport his body, big for a boy, along the roads and over the fields of the idle valley.

When he was fifteen years of age he began to know fame, local fame and for limited exploits, but afterwards he said that that rural reputation touched him with a higher joy than all that was ever said about him in cities or written about him in reviews when he had grown to manhood and the making of books.

That autumn evening in Jack Stuart's orchard in Towney he knew no contradiction. Life narrowed down to one exploit and one aim. Running around the orchard, hopping from tree to tree, trailing after him in the grass the tail of a grown man's coat, worn because of its capacious pockets, stuffing those pockets with exquisitely crisp fruit, he was the hero among his companions. Even when his foot suffered from Jack Stuart's devilish system of 'snakes,' man-traps and spring-guns, the tragedy only added to the elevation of Billy Carleton and meant the discomfiture and disgrace of the ingenious Jack.

It was the beginning of a great career, glorious idleness, daredevil deeds that endeared him to his people, leading him on into an intimacy with them in which he knew all the elusive, evasive undertones of their lives, the secret language of their hearts. 'No dance missed me,' he wrote. 'I was perpetually leaping, and throwing the stone and the sledge. No football match was without me. I

[1] 'Father Butler.'

16

have gone five miles to wakes and dances. We had not only what were known as common dances in those days, but we had what were politely called balls. The difference between a ball and a common dance was this. At the ball we had whisky. . . . There was then, indeed, great simplicity of manners, and a number of those old, hereditary virtues which had their origin in the purity and want of guile which consecrated domestic life. During all my association with these pastimes and harmless amusements, I never knew a single instance of a female coming to shame or loss of character.'[1] Perpetually leaping, playing the strong man, dancing at common dances, dancing and drinking whisky and purchasing whisky for the ladies at polite balls—all the time he was learning the people, their oddities and evils and simplicities and purities.

In 1850 in London he saw Ben Caunt the pugilist, a powerful pugilist and a mighty man, but neither as powerful or mighty as Frank Farrel who kept the mill in Clogher back in those days of sunshine and idleness. Looking at fighting Ben he remembered Frank and the great strength made harmless by innate amiability, remembered the day he went with his brother James down to the mill where Carleton's corn was being ground. In the old, tottering building 'white with mealy cobwebs' the gigantic miller congratulated him on his reputation for athletics. They stood under the great beam that, by all appearances, held the crazy building together, and Frank Farrel, displaying his strength, pitched a half hundred-weight clear over the beam, dared Billy to follow his example. Out of the tail of his eye young Carleton saw a lad called Dickey running to tell the town of Clogher and, rejoicing in the wonder and admiration of those who returned with Dickey, he used all his skill and strength, flung the weight, surpassed even Frank Farrel. Afterwards, in the dusty air of the mill, they drank good poteen, and the story of his strength went out to add to the reputation he had made the day he leaped the river at Clogher Karry with the whole world watching him. The whole world called the place Carleton's Leap, and the name remained for many a long year after that great event. 'There I stood,' he said, 'a fine, well-dressed young fellow, in my twenty-first year; an individual from whom great things were expected—yet what would I be in a week? A working-man, no better than one of themselves, with a paper cap on my head and a coarse apron before me.'[2]

For his eldest brother Michael, with a tongue bitterer than the tongue of Timon of Athens, had suggested to him that instead of perpetually dancing, dreaming, leaping rivers and tossing weights, he should go and find himself a trade. When he raced over the

1 O'Donoghue, vol. i, p. 93.
2 O'Donoghue, vol. i, p. 117.

17

rustling grass, leaped over the calm water, he must have felt that the leap might carry him further than the other side of the river, might carry him onwards out of the valley for ever. He was lazy and loved idleness. But even more than that, his heart must have clung to the stability of a life in which a young man had to make no decision, in which everything was as definite as a race and a leap or the upward swing of a strong arm throwing a weight, everything as sweet as stolen apples, as gay as a dance, as exquisitely coloured as the hills and hedges of the valley. He was holding desperately to delicious days that always afterwards filled at least five-sixths of his heart.

TWO

VERY UNDERSTANDABLY Brother Michael was not impressed by the fact that William read the classics several hours every day. They were poor people. Michael had to work. Reading the classics was not work. It might be all right for the gentry. It could be a pastime for priests. William's father had wanted to see his son a priest. But William had apparently other ideas or no ideas; and, as Michael saw it, a man could be only one of two things, a priest or a working-man. Nevertheless, William read the classics. William pursued books. William went to school.

He went to school for the first time when he was six or seven years of age, and his people lived in the townland of Towney. That morning he had never even seen a letter of the alphabet. Coming home in the evening he had mastered the entire twenty-six letters and could even spell the word 'bag.' But that one initiatory day of scholarship had done something more notable for him than introduce him to an arbitrary arrangement of symbols. It had shown him the hedge-schoolmaster, the king of all hedge-schoolmasters who had been, also, in his young days a poor scholar: Pat Frayne from Connaught. And in later years, when Carleton sat down to write, Pat Frayne took upon him the garment of immortality, became Mat Kavanagh, Philomath and Professor of the Learned Languages, ready to teach book-keeping by single and double entry, geometry, trigonometry, stereometry, mensuration, navigation, gauging, surveying, dialling, astronomy, astrology, austerity and fluxions; or in the classics everything from Aesop's fables and the colloquies of Erasmus to Cornelius Agrippa and Cholera Morbus; or anything from Greek Grammar to Irish radically and a small taste of Hebrew upon the Masoretic text.[1]

Mat's or Pat's past as a poor scholar, his present pretensions as a man of learning and a maker of scholars, went by in that one day like the flash of a meteor. For when Pat saw that Towney sent only three boys to follow learning at his feet he moved on in disgust to enlighten some other townland, returning later to Skelgy, to a school-house scooped out of the bank on the side of the road where he sat in glory in the centre of a circle of a hundred boys and girls. One lad in the circle was never to forget his teacher, nor allow him to be forgotten. He was an urchin like the other urchins, sitting on the bare earth, stretching speckled shins 'like sausages on a *Poloni* dish' towards the heat of the turf-fire. He was, maybe, as tattered as his neighbours: one with half a thigh absent from his breeches,

1 'The Hedge School' (*Traits and Stories*).

19

another with an arm missing from his coat, a third with no breeches at all but covering his loins with his mother's old petticoat, a fourth with no coat, a fifth wearing a cap to cover the scald he got when he sat under the juice dripping from fresh bacon, a sixth with a black eye, a seventh with rags under his heels to keep his kibes clean, 'an eighth crying to get home, because he has got a headache, though it may be as well to hint that there is a drag-hunt to start from beside his father's in the course of the day.' They were the sons and daughters of a ragged, hungry people, still caring enough about learning to pursue it in spite of rags and in spite of hunger. On them Pat Frayne or Mat Kavanagh was to exercise his tumbled, twisted fragments of wisdom, pedantry, conceit, poetry, eloquence, big words robbed recklessly from half-understood books, big ideas with joints swollen and crippled from unwise and inopportune use. And in the circle and at the mercy of that chaotic outpouring of pedantic things was Billy Carleton, learning, his father hoped, to be a priest, beginning very dimly to realise that words were good and desirable.

For one thing, long words made the people look up to you, a delicious thing for a vain young man. The savour of such words was sweet on the tongue; the learned language of the philomaths was, as Hycy Burke said of the letter written by schoolmaster Finigan who had also in his soul much of schoolmaster Frayne, like the land of Canaan, flowing in milk and honey.[1] What Finigan. thought of Hycy serves both as a sample of the elegant style and an excellent introduction to the whole class of would-be gentlemen. 'Fame, Mr. Burke,' said Finigan, 'has not been silent with regard to your exploits. Your horsemanship, sir, and the intrepid pertinacity with which you fasten upon the reluctant society of men of rank have given you a notorious celebrity. . . . And you shine, Mr. Burke, in the loves as well as in the—*tam veneri quam*—I was about to add *Marti*, but it would be inappropriate, or might only remind you of poor Biddy Martin, on whom you have, in an illegitimate sense, conferred the character of maternity. It is well known that you are a most accomplished gentleman, Mr. Burke— *homo factus ad unguem—ad unguem.*'

Taking his place in the tattered circle the boy was beginning something that was to absorb much of his energy, much of his time: a hungry search for wisdom, a joy in mere verbiage right up to his ecstasy, which was also the ecstasy of Denis O'Shaughnessy,[2] in strutting about the country uttering sesquipedalian words. At the beginning of all that, was the extraordinary figure of Pat Frayne. There were other schools and other teachers. A year after Pat's one

---
[1] *The Emigrants of Ahadarra.*
[2] 'Denis O'Shaughnessy Going to Maynooth' (*Traits and Stories*).

20

day in Towney, Mrs. Dumont, an Irishwoman whose French husband had perished in the revolution, came with her daughter to the townland of Kark and opened a school in Jack Stuart's barn. Tall, aged, dressed in black, 'she had the bearing of an empress. She took snuff, and talked French to her daughter. In blood she was half Maguire from Fermanagh and half O'Donnell from Donegal, and Carleton was near enough to the past to pay attention to such things. She enjoyed universal respect. Even the wealthiest Protestants and Presbyterians raised their hats to her. 'Priest and parson treated her as if she was the lady of the land.' But in spite of all this, in spite of his eight-year old attachment for Mary Anne Dumont young Billy went with reluctance to his lessons in Stuart's barn. The knowledge of his own backwardness troubled him. Then one day a taunt from a girl somewhat older than himself led to explosion and open battle while Mrs. Dumont was temporarily absent, and ignominious expulsion when Mrs. Dumont suddenly returned.

Then up in Findramore there was another Connaught man called O'Beirne, an excellent teacher, and a good book-keeper, the right qualities for a man in his profession but no claims on glorious, poteen-worshipping, word-worshipping immortality. Later, when one of many removals brought the Carletons to paradisal Nurchasy, he walked his bare-footed way to a new, classical school in the townland of Tulnavert, to suffer under a brute of a man who 'should have been kept closely confined in a lunatic asylum during his life,' but who, after his death, found his way into the pages of *The Poor Scholar*. Later still there was McGoldrick the classical teacher; and Wiley, a Presbyterian clergyman, a Trinity College graduate, but a dwarf who 'in or out of hell was matchless for savage brutality;' and Carleton's cousin Keenan who moved uneasily in and out of his life for several years.

All shadows and nonentities and insubstantial things when compared with Mat sitting on his deal chair, stretching his legs in a lordly manner, wearing his hat, surveying his tattered hundred, enjoying the sweet delirium of authority. His own black coat was not without a blemish. His white cravat was streaked with brown where it came into contact with his chin. But in his hand was a large broad ruler 'the emblem of his power, the woeful instrument of executive justice, and the signal of terror to all within his jurisdiction.' On his tongue were words, learned words, thundering words, his own antidote against his own deficiencies, his principal defence against scholars who could at times be unruly enough to bolt and bar him out of his own subterranean schoolhouse, against patrons who could love learning to the excessive point of kidnapping the teacher and carrying him off to open a school in their own townland. Even kidnappers would respect a man who, coming out of a drugged sleep, could cry out for water in these words. 'I'm all in a state of conflagration; and my head—by the sowl of Newton, the inventor of fluxions, but my head is a complete illucidation of the centrifugle motion. . . . Nancy, I say, for God's sake, quicken yourself wid the hydraulics, or the best mathematician in Ireland's gone to the abode of Euclid and Pythagoras, that first invented the multiplication table.' A spelling lesson with Mat Kavanagh could have all the delight and the unexpectedness of high poetry. 'Silence boys,' he would roar, 'till I spell Nebachodnazure for Paddy Magouran. Listen; and you yourself, Paddy, are one of the letters:

> A turf and a *clod* spells Nebachod—
> A knife and a razure spells Nebachodnazure—
> Three pair of boots and five pairs of shoes
> Spells Nebachodnazure the King of the Jews.'

For Plato himself had been a hedge-schoolmaster, seeking truth and expounding truth in 'a nate little spot in Greece, called the Groves of Academus'; and the druids taught under the oaks; and in the Garden of Eden there had been the Tree of Knowledge. Mat and a teaching colleague could confound a visitor from Cambridge by laying emphasis thus on the honourable precedents for hedge-schoolmastering, or by presenting him with posers that would have staggered the most intricately flippant of the later Scholastics. Could he find the solid contents of a load of thorns? Could he do the Snail? Could he do A and B on opposite sides of a wood, without the key? Or maybe, and at this stage Mat's colleague would throw off his frieze jock to display a great muscular body, maybe the visiting gentleman would like 'a small taste of the Scuffle.'

For his patrons frequently expected from the hedge-schoolmaster something above and beyond the mere routine of scholasticism. To know the three sets of book-keeping or a verse of bog-Latin like:

> *Regibus et clotibus solemus stopere windous,*
> *Nos numerus sumus fruges consumere nati,*
> *Stercora flat stire rara terra-tantaro bungo,*

was praiseworthy, liberal knowledge. But to know how to attack and defend with a well-chosen, well-seasoned blackthorn was utilitarian knowledge. The Findramore men who kidnapped Mat Kavanagh mentioned, in their previous public advertisement for a schoolmaster, that a knowledge of cudgel-fencing would be an added qualification 'but (he) mustn't tache us with a staff that bends in the middle, bekase it breaks one's head across the guard.' And in Paddy Mulligan's school,[1] which could again have been Pat

---

[1] 'The Party Fight and Funeral' (*Traits and Stories*).

22

Frayne's school, the boys studied mostly the art of oiling and seasoning sticks, boring a hole in the lower end with a red-hot iron spindle, filling the hole with melted lead, and using the product in battle, in preparation for the more serious conflicts that would come with man's years.

Sylvester Maguire, a poet quoted by one of the learning-hungry men from Findramore, had written at least one quatrain—as every poet should—in praise of learning.

> *Labour for larnin' before you grow old,*
> *For larnin' is better nor riches nor gould;*
> *Riches an' gould they may vanish away,*
> *But larnin' alone it will never decay.*

But O'Shaughran the schoolmaster in *The Squanders of Castle Squander* sang the praises of something more potent than wisdom:

> *There's great old Homer, that fine old poemer,*
> *'Twasn't in St. Omer's he sucked it in:*
> *The thundering rhymer, got always a primer*
> *From copious draughts of the true poteen.*

And somewhere between the sentiments expressed in the two jingles were the heart and loyalty of Mat Kavanagh. For as the Findramore men saw it, learning, drink, and lunacy went together; and no sensible citizen would send his children to be educated by such a schoolmaster as Mat Meegan 'that dry-headed dunce, with his black coat upon him and his caroline hat, and him wouldn't taste a glass of poteen wanst in seven years.' A sober, black-coated man would not be over-willing to play learned clerk to some of the nefarious, nocturnal activities of the bright boys of the place. But a scholar who drank and understood the cudgels had spirit enough, natural and infused, for any devilment under the moon. Mat Kavanagh was eventually reprieved off the very scaffold, proclaiming that he died at peace with all men except the men of Findramore 'whom may the male-dictionary execration of a dying man follow into eternal infinity,' and leaving his manuscript of conic sections to some person or persons unknown. For pardon and reprieve interrupted his dying speech and ended Carleton's story. Many schoolmasters had actually ended on the scaffold, and Carleton knew it. Mat Kavanagh could not die, because he was with the immortals, because he had so much in him of Pat Frayne from Connaught who had passed once through the Clogher Valley, passed on possibly into 'eternal infinity.' But in the eyes of a boy he had left for ever a vision of that crowded underground schoolroom, of learning still dignified

23

in spite of rags and tatters. In the ears of a boy he had left for ever the echo of words run wild, comically awry, at times spavined and humped-backed, but always alive with a humorous and exalted vitality.

In the valleys of far away Kerry were the echoes of a lost learning and a dying poetry. The shadows of bitter-tongued Egan O'Rahilly, or drunken, wandering Owen O'Sullivan, or the gallant Piaras Ferriter that the Cromwellians had hanged in Killarney town, still stirred uneasily among the people of the Munster mountains. The past was stronger there than anywhere else in Ireland; and the past meant schools and learning, the echoes of Gaelic verse, the languages of Greece and Rome. If a boy seriously wanted to follow learning he must follow it along the road that led to Munster, and, as a general rule, along the road that led to the priesthood.

There was nothing specifically priestly, nothing specifically scholarly about that big, growing, athletic, light-hearted boy. Pat Frayne failed to make him a mathematician and never during his life was William Carleton, characteristically enough, able to work out a proposition of Euclid. He was head of the class, though, in Pat Frayne's rather original spelling lessons. Those lessons ended the work of the day. Each boy put down a pin and the winner went home, his coat-sleeve shining silver with the pins won by accurate spelling, and, day after day the winner was William Carleton. But in spite of his prowess in spelling words and accumulating pins it was his brother John that his father sent to the new classical school at Aughentain in the hope that he had in him the makings of a priest. Brother John who, under Pat Frayne, had added and subtracted with the best of them, revolted from the classics like a shy horse from mystery. William would have been sent in his place, but the school at Aughentain had been as impermanent as most such schools, and William 'nicely smoothed up by a new suit of clothes' had nowhere to go.

Later he turned his eyes to scholarly Munster where the schools had higher reputations and longer lives. His father had gone to his grave in the churchyard in Clogher, followed by the 'largest funeral concourse remembered in the parish,' taking with him to the dust his simple and easily explainable ambition to see one of his sons wearing the robes of a priest. Afterwards, in dark moments, he could write in a superior fashion of his father's prayers and piety, of his desire to have a son ordained, and in a bitter enough way about priests and the priesthood. But when life was easier and the darkness gave way to light and the echoes of his mother's songs were in his soul he could say: 'It has always been the ambition, and an honourable ambition, too, of the Irish Roman Catholic of the peasant class, to make his son a priest.'[1] His own ambition was, also, simple enough and easily explainable, but very different from his father's. But when he set off southwards on the road to Munster he hadn't started to analyse or at least to write the record of his own approach to the priesthood. Later he came as near to analysing it as a man who had never succeeded in mastering a proposition of Euclid could come to analysing anything.

One morning a man called Pat McArdle came over to Carleton's house. He was a man past thirty years of age, 'better dressed in his suit of black than his uncle the priest himself,' but to his uncle and the Carletons and the world he said he was bound for Munster as a poor scholar, his ultimate destination the priesthood. He had a brother in Maynooth. On the strength of his high aspirations he borrowed fifty pounds from his clerical uncle. On the strength of his clerical connections he suggested to James Carleton that William's purse should be placed in his keeping for the duration of their journey to learned Munster. James was unresponsive and the priest's nephew moved off, possibly also to 'eternal infinity,' leaving William Carleton to follow his journey alone. He never reached Kerry. Randy O'Rollick's eulogy of that county[2] was as far as Carleton was concerned only the comic condensation of the gossip of a country that respected learning and the abode of learning, whether in Trinity College or in a cabin in Kerry. 'Kerry,' said Randy, 'is the most classical county in Ireland. Latin is the vernacular language of the schoolboys; wherever you go, you will hear them talking Latin to each other, and singing the Odes of Horace, as they sit behind the creels upon the horses, while drawing their turf. At every sizarship examination in Trinity College . . . nineteen out of every twenty of them come from that indoctrinated and classical county. But at Grehan's inn at Granard, less than halfway to all that classicism and doctrine, the boy had a dream about a bull, a mad bull, chasing him to gore him. In the morning he turned northwards towards home, pursued possibly by that dream-bull, back up the hilly road to Springtown as if he was treading on air, back to a welcome by his people who had been sorry since he had left. It was not so much that he had turned his back on Munster as that he had turned his face again to the warm, quiet valley of home.

It was a very imperfect experience. But like so many human things that are unfinished and imperfect it gave the initial impulse to the artistic making of something complete and perfect, to the telling of the exquisite story of Jemmy McEvoy, the poor scholar, who made the long journey to Munster, who persevered and became

[1] *The Red-Haired Man's Wife.*
[2] *The Squanders of Castle Squander.*

25

a priest, who symbolised a whole people when he walked through famine and fever in the valley of the shadow of death. Into that story he wrote much of what he had seen, more of what he had heard. On the side of the hard, barren hill of Esker Dhu, Jemmy and his father Dominick dig the potatoes, suffering as well as they can the bitter wind and the sleety rain, looking down on the sheltered valley and the cosy farm from which they had been wrongfully evicted, the father consoling himself with the prophecy of Pastorini that when 'Twenty-five comes, *we'll* have our own again: the right will overcome the might—the bottomless pit will be locked. There was a great deal of Carleton in the wild gesture with which young Jemmy pitched his spade to the wind and slavery to the devil, a great deal of his mixed ideas on vocation to the priesthood in Jemmy's vow to go to Munster and learn Latin, to return and raise and restore his people to their lawful place, to bring down Yellow Sam, the evicting agent, who was born without a heart, who carried black wool in his ears to deaden the cries of widows and orphans long rotten in the grave through his villainy. But those mixed and muddled ideas were very close to the heart of a patient and impoverished people, as close as Jemmy the wandering scholar was to the hearts of those who befriended him on the road, who fought his battle against the insane cruelty of the schoolmaster, who brought him help when he fell down and lay in a ditch, weak with hunger and burning with fever. For the people loved him because he was poor, because he followed learning, because he aspired to the priesthood; and, outweighing all the bitter things written in black moments, is the vision of poor Jemmy walking the length of Ireland and treated by the people as if he was a haloed saint.

The satchel of books on his back was the only pass he needed into the hearts of the people. In the words of the kind and loquacious schoolmaster that Jemmy met on the way to Munster it was the 'badge of polite genius that no boy need be ashamed of.' And Munster was, according to the same pedagogue, the land where the swallows fly in conic sections, where magpies and turkeys confab in Latin, where cows and bullocks roar in Doric Greek. So Jemmy McEvoy, or Jemmy Donnelly as he was in real life, went his way to the lost land of learning, like the fortunate third son in the rhythm of the ancient folk-tales, endured suffering and acquired learning, returned 'a priest and a gentleman' with powerful friends who saw Yellow Sam humbled and the poor restored to their rightful possessions. The ending had also all the pleasant poetic justice of the ancient stories; and all through his life Carleton had the tendency of the senachie to give his story the twist that would send it upwards to the stars. When he wrote in *The Black Prophet* about the devastation of famine, when he wrote in *The Emigrants of Ahadarra* of the

26

way in which Ireland was bleeding to death by emigration, he saw to it that the good people whose stories the books told neither died of hunger nor sailed westwards into mystery and a new world. In the same way Jemmy McEvoy made the journey there and back and saw the wishes of his heart fulfilled. But William Carleton turned back at Granard in the Irish Midlands and came home hotfoot, pursued by a bull that roared out of his dreams. Possibly he came back because he had in him much more of Denis O'Shaughnessy than of Jemmy McEvoy; and Denis O'Shaughnessy, who awed the country by his long words and his high talk of going to Maynooth, endured the life of that college only for a very brief time. The reason was because Denis O'Shaughnessy had in him so much of William Carleton. Behind all the fun and delightful idleness there was unease and indetermination, a feeling that outside the valley the round earth was unsteady under the feet.

THREE

DENIS O'SHAUGHNESSY'S[1] call to a clerical life was part intoxication in words for the sake of words, part a superiority feeling that made him accept the admiration of the people as his lawful right and 'condimnate' his father as a 'most ungrammatical ould man' unfit to argue with anyone who knew Murray's English Grammar and the three concords of Lilly's Latin Grammar. Part, also, was base material calculation. Surrounded by the worship of his parents, brothers and sisters, he drew for his own and their delectation an airy vision of the days to come when he should reign in power as a parish priest. His parishioners would never be late with their dues and, tame as mice before his might, they would provide him with enough yarn every year to clothe three regiments of militia, or, even, dragoons. He would hold his stations in the snuggest farmhouses in the parish. He would talk liberally to the Protestant boddaghs, give the Presbyterians a learned homily on civil and religious liberty and make hard hits with them about the incubus of an established church, so that from many of both creeds he would fill bag after bag of good corn. Speculatively Denis considered whether or not his sister Susy would have the accomplishments necessary in a parish priest's cook. Could she dress a dinner for a bishop? Could she make pies and puddings and disport her fancy through all the varieties of roast and boil? How would she dress a fowl so that it would stand on a dish as if it were going to dance a hornpipe? How would she 'amalgamate the different *genera* of wine with boiling fluid and crystallised saccharine matter?' How would she dispose of the various dishes on the table according to high life and mathematics?

Father Denis of that imagined future would rise up in the morning, read part of his office, ride out with his curate, '*ego et coadjutor meus,*' or if more fortunate with his two curates, all mounted on their horses 'as gracefully as three throopers.' In a world in which the dew sparkled under the morning sun, the crows cawed melodiously the three 'reverend sentimentalists' would advance 'gazing with odoriferous admiration upon the prospect about us, and expatiating in the purest of Latin upon the beauties of unsophisticated nature.' The clerical boots of the parish priest would be 'as brilliant as the countenance of Phoebus when decked with rosy smiles.' The boots worn by the curates would be 'more subordinately polished.' On the 'anterior rotundity' of the superior cleric the sun would reflect from a bunch of gold seals; but the curates could

[1] 'Denis O'Shaughnessy Going to Maynooth' (*Traits and Stories*).

sport only a poor ribbon and a twopenny key. Their destination would be the house of a wealthy farmer. Their purpose the hearing of confessions and the reading of Mass. But as Denis saw it in radiant prospect the main event of the day was the station-dinner; and in a passion of prophetic eloquence he invoked before his puzzled, worshipping family circle the 'pagan professors of eating and drinking.' The list of powers appealed to would have tuned in with the zeal of Pico Della Mirandola in reconciling Christianity and Hellenism: Bacchus, Epicurus and St. Heliogabulus; Anthony of Padua and Paul the Hermit 'who poached for his own venison;' St. Tuck and St. Tak'em, St. Drinkem and St. Eatem.

No doubt Denis O'Shaughnessy knew high joy in looking forward to the parish priest that he was never to be. William Carleton's joy in looking back to the Denis O'Shaughnessy that he had been, must have been mixed with other complicated and not completely pleasant feelings. He knew the giant laughter that must underlie always the creation and contemplation of such a naive humbug as Denis. He knew also the pain that a mother might suddenly feel even when sharing the laughter of her child. Laughing at Denis he remembered and laughed at his own youth and his own folly. A man could indulge in no more healthful exercise. But it must have twisted something in the part of his own soul that remembered the past to use even his own sanative laughter at himself as a subtle satire on the eating powers of priests. William Carleton the boy, and Denis O'Shaughnessy did really think that the call to the priesthood was little more than a call to the dinner-table. Well and good for Denis who left Maynooth anyway and went back home to marry the girl he had loved all the time. It was not so good for William. He never reached Maynooth, but he lived to write a lot about those who did, who studied there, who returned as priests to a hungry people. No doubt many of them being men were fond of their food. But it was William Carleton's misfortune that he, when he started to write, was a hungry man, also fond of his food; that food was offered to him on condition that he perverted the comic prayer of Denis to the pagan professors of the table into a serious, universal charge against the priests. He was even required to carry this debasing of his genius to the point of an accusation of sin and superstition and the worshipping of false gods.

The parsonage house was, according to Archbishop Whately, the nucleus of civilisation in remote parts of Ireland. That was possibly very true from Archbishop Whately's point of view, for civilisation is relative, and when the mass of the people are poor and un-educated in the modern sense, the type of civilisation that is founded on money and regular schooling will necessarily be very much detached from the mass of the people. Even when the parson in nineteenth-century Ireland was not separate and apart from the people, the parsonage was. It may have been a quiet, refined, cultured, civilised place but, in spite of Archbishop Whately, it was not the nucleus of civilisation. It was not the nucleus of anything. It was a high house on a hill, an avenue leading up to it, graciously ringed by tall trees. But the man who lived there was infinitely further away from the hearts of the people than even a mere rollicking priest like Lever's Father Malachy Duggan or the galloping priest, in Lover's *Rory O'More*, who loved to take a dart after the hounds.

Rollicking and galloping are not necessarily priestly or highly spiritual occupations, but they are human and civilised, and the priest could be at the heart of them and still remain a priest. The priest could also be first in the fight when the mad spirit rose in a broken, cowed people; and the soldiery, who still further crushed the people and restored the civilisation of which the parsonage was the nucleus, could burn a priest in a fire so that his followers could fill their nostrils 'with the smell of roasted priest.' They did that, round about the time William Carleton was born into a people who had lived for centuries under a shadow. Living with them in the darkness, sharing their most intense sufferings, was the priest. Before Carleton died, priest and people were together on the high road from gloom to brightness. The people were shaking the barriers built not about the parsonage but about the landlord's big house. The people did not always agree with the priests as to what barriers should be broken, nor what weapons should be used to break them. But their long association in suffering naturally gave the priest an influence over the people that the parson in the civilised parsonage never possessed. At times it could be an undue influence because a priest was a man. But the priest could also be a martyr; and William Carleton who, when he was Denis O'Shaughnessy, had looked forward to the priesthood for comically unworthy motives, had still enough clear vision in him to see the high dignity of the office, to see that it bore a fixed relation to something noble in the people, to see that it could be approached for worthy as well as unworthy motives. So the priests walk through his pages, worthy and unworthy, good and bad, happy and unfortunate. The pity is, that because of his own uncertain, chaotic story men coming after have been inclined to read only one meaning into the stories that he told.

When the priest of his own home parish appealed to the parishioners for funds to set Jemmy Donnelly—or Jemmy McEvoy—on the road to Munster, Billy Carleton saw easily enough the influence that the priest and the religion he represented had over the people. They responded to the appeal not only because their own charitable instincts were touched but also because it was a religious duty. 'There was not a single prejudice, or weakness, or virtue in the disposition of his auditory left untouched in this address. He moved their superstition, their pride of character, their dread of hell and purgatory, their detestation of Yellow Sam, and the remembrance of the injury inflicted on McEvoy's family; he glanced at the advantage to be derived from the lad's prayers, the example they should set to Protestants, made a passing hit at tithes, and indulged in the humorous, the pathetic and the miraculous.'[1] This type of sermon, he pointed out, was a sample of the uncouth, powerful eloquence that prevailed before the establishment of Maynooth, when 'in consequence of the dearth of priests' men were admitted to orders straight from the hedge-schools, some even ordained before they left for continental colleges to be educated 'in order that they might, by saying masses and performing other clerical duties, be enabled to add something to the scanty pittance which was appropriated to their support.'

The pity was that the analytic comment on that particular sermon, the much less analytic comments on other sermons and the men that preached them and the lives they lived, were not written down when he had the single, free mind of a boy. There in the valley he saw his own people face-to-face, heard their words as clearly as labourers in a field could hear the voice of a neighbour blessing their work as he passed along the road. But in later years, in his years of writing, the vision at times could be dim, the words spoken, broken and indistinct; for in between was the misery of angry years and the influence of one man frenziedly hating the faith that made up so much of the life of Carleton's people. Priests and pilgrims, shrines and patterns, places of worship that changed in his own lifetime from rocky corners in glens or bare slopes on mountains to solidly built buildings, all these evidences of the faith of the people were part of his boyhood and young manhood. He wanted to be a priest. He was for a while a pilgrim, setting out barefoot to cross the mountains to Petigo and pray where tradition said St. Patrick had prayed on an island in a cold lake. Later he wrote that what he saw on that pilgrimage killed for ever his desire to be a priest, even turned him away from the faith in which his parents had lived and died. But it is unsafe to accept his evidence, unsafe even to go with him and see what he saw on that pilgrimage, until a longer road to the south has taken him to the city of Dublin, brought him into the presence of a strange creature called Caesar Otway. That lean clergyman, turning suddenly from his Bible, his antipopery pamphlets, his love of travelling, his exquisite writing of prose, had perception enough to see that in this poverty-stricken

[1] 'The Poor Scholar' (*Traits and Stories*).

31

peasant with a dozen grudges he had uncovered good propagandist material. He may or may not have seen that he had also discovered a genius.

It was poverty and pride and the reading of a book drove him finally away from the valley. When he was nine or ten years of age he was hunting the neighbours' houses for books, fascinated, possibly, by the miracle of binding, fluttering leaves, printed words that he was only partially able to decipher. Books were not plentiful and the most diligent dint of searching might result only in an odd volume of a novel, a fragment of a story like a voice speaking out of another life and fading away before the words were distinctly heard. The drama touched him passingly in Jack Stuart's barn where the people, remembering the past, performed crude plays about the siege of Derry and the battle of Aughrim. He was in there among the 'multitudes,' both Catholic and Protestant, who crowded to see the play-actors. At the age of ten he was stage-director and prompter to amateurs of both religions. He knew word for word the whole play about the battle of Aughrim. There was a ghost in that drama, and one summer night when the audience watched breathlessly the spectral appearance, the barnfloor collapsed, and sacks of barley, playgoers, prompter and players and ghost and stage-properties descended with a crash on the patient cattle in Jack Stuart's byre. There were no deaths.

At Tulnavert school one day he struck up a friendship with a lad called William Short, accepted his friend's invitation to spend a few days holidaying in the Short household. The two lads went out of the valley, up a mountain road to the place where Short's father owned wide acres of mountain-land and had, mysteriously enough, become a wealthy man. In that house he found and read 'with wonder' an odd volume of *Tom Jones*.

Another day he was working with the men drowning flax. With his natural laziness he lay down comfortably among the bundles as they were tumbled out of the cart that carried them to the side of the flax-pond; and in that green comfort, while others worked, he read until his heart remembered it forever *Amoranda, or The Reformed Coquette*—how she would be admired by all men but would love or be loved by one, how on the continent she found again the only man who had touched her heart. Around him as he read men worked and talked, cartwheels rattled, the dogs barked, the green bundles splashed into the water. But he was away on the coloured continent with Amoranda the lovely lady and her venerable friend who suddenly, disposing with a gesture of a wig and a false nose, revealed himself as her true love. He followed romance through the pages of the Arabian Nights. He read, also, the *Life*

32

of Edward, Lord Herbert and Defoe's *History of the Devil.* Even in houses where the people could not read English he found in shadowy places behind the hearth, or in dusty corners under the rafters, or tucked away behind plates on the dressers, books and pamphlets and the inevitable odd volume of a novel. He found wisdom and knowledge in almanacks and magazines. He heard the echoes of the songs of Burns, and made them sound again through the story[1] of Willy Martley, the blind musician, whose favourite tune was the one to which the words of *Jean* moved melodiously. But, always, he had from books only the crumbs and gatherings of knowledge as mixed and muddled as the volumes the neighbours brought as presents to Denis O'Shaughnessy when they heard the good news that he soon was actually going to Maynooth. One brought him *The Necessity of Penance,* another gave him *Laugh And Be Fat,* a third *The Key of Paradise,* a fourth the cheering alternative entitled *Hell Open.* The library included the *Irish Rogues and Rapparees,* Butler's *Lives of the Saints, The Necessity of Fasting* and *The Epicure's Vade Mecum,* the *Garden of Love and Royal Flower of Fidelity,* a volume on the virtue of celibacy, a very much out-of-place volume of statistics about the population of Ireland, *The Devil Upon Two Sticks* and a biography of St. Anthony.

'Take these Misther Denis,' said the kind people, 'they're of no use to us, at all at all; but they'll sarve you, of coorse, where you're goin', bekase when you want books in the college you can use them.'

With something of the same generous gesture the poor people surrendered to the prowling Carleton boy the books they had treasured more for their symbolic significance than for any proved utility. He took them and read them and was still unsatisfied, for he wanted, all the time, to study the classics. His precarious schooling led him eventually through the first four books of Virgil and he professed himself touched to tears by the death of Dido—an unusual reaction for a schoolboy. He read the classics or, at least he read these few school-texts as novels, not as combinations of grammatical puzzles; he read them through his imagination, not through his judgment. He read them, also, because in his own mind and in the mind of those around him the language of the ancient world was part of the indispensable accoutrement of the learned man. He wanted passionately to be a man of learning; he also needed to eat. The voice of his father who had told stories, the sweet singing voice of his mother were quiet forever in the grave. Relatives wearied easily of the lithe, strong fellow who read books, talked big words, avoided honest labour and seemed to regard himself as called to some especially high destiny. The pose was acceptable when the high

[1] 'The Clarionet.'

33

destiny was presumed to be the priesthood, for a clerical relative was no loss to any family. But books and big words buttered no bread, and brother Michael looked down his nose at lazy, learned William, and very pointedly suggested work. For a few days he cut stone or talked about the classics in the workshop of his friend Lanty Doain, the stone-cutter; and Lanty taking down a book read out a passage from Justin, and together they agreed that *praefectus ipius prepositus mediis* meant something like: Lord Lieutenant over the Medes. Lanty considered that, as far as classicism went, he had got himself an exceptional apprentice; William considered that Lanty was something more than a common stonecutter. Still he went home in dull humour. He said: 'I became misanthropical. I detested the world. Everything went against me and my family. The latter, among whom, of course, I was forced to include myself, were almost beggars, and nothing for me, in the shape of any opening in the future, offered itself except the hard shapeless granite—the chisel and the mallet. I could almost have pitched myself down a precipice.'[1]

He didn't. But about that time he borrowed a book from a packman. The author of the book was a Frenchman. The hero was a Spanish lad who left his native Santillane to go studying in Salamanca, but fell among thieves and began a life of coloured adventure and roguery and dry, detached comment on men and the ways of men. The genius of Gil Blas for living, the creative, writing genius of Le Sage, possibly in Tobias Smollett's translation, came like a vision to a young man in an Irish valley, showing him suddenly the whole whirling, inconsequential world of the picaresque; and he thought every word of it as true as the gospel of St. John.

'Shall I buy a short cassock,' said Gil Blas to himself, 'and go to Salamanca to set up for a tutor? Why should I adopt the costume of a licentiate? For the purpose of going into orders? Do I feel an inward call? No. If I have any call, it is quite the contrary way. I had rather wear a sword than an apron; and push my fortune in this world, before I think of the next.'[2] They were honeyed words for a young fellow who didn't want to work, whose relatives could not or would not support him in idleness. It was ecstasy to think of the world open before you, ripe for plunder, to read that Fate equally thrust footmen and heroes into the world, to imagine wild adventures with robbers, wild nights with actors and actresses, high life in courts and palaces. There was example for it. It had all happened to a fellow in Spain. Was Doctor Sangrado, bringing all his patients

[1] O'Donoghue, vol. i.

[2] *The Adventures of Gil Blas of Santillane.* Translated from the French of Le Sage by Tobias Smollett (Routledge and Sons, London).

to an easy end by phlebotomy and the administering of drinks of pure water, a patch or a shadow of Barney Bradley,[1] barber and surgeon to man and beast, whose parish was the best-bled parish in Europe, who administered liberally burnt whiskey and Glauber salts, who called his craft 'flaybottomry'? Mat Kavanagh had never turned from pedagogy to the writing of tragedy; but had he had the time, the opportunity, the background, the inspiration, he might easily have surpassed the effort that Signor Thomas presented to the burgesses of Olmedo. In that pageant the King of Morocco followed the high tradition of tragedy, shooting a hundred Moorish slaves with arrows merely by way of diversion, beheading thirty Portuguese officers, and, weary with the stress and strain of domestication, burning his entire seraglio.

Words and sentences and episodes may have leaped out like that as the fascinated young man followed through forty changes of fortune the progress of Master Gil Blas to worldly glory. The cave of the robbers in which Gil Blas was imprisoned, in which he heard all the maxims of knavery, from which he rescued the high-born widow, was certainly one of the great caves in literature and in human history. It had its influence on the cave to which Carleton followed the rapparees when he wrote the story of Redmond Count O'Hanlon, on the cave in which he saw the persecuted priests of penal times when he wrote the story of Willy Reilly and his own dear Cooleen Bawn. Carleton always retained the romantic love of the boy for such things. It had all happened. It was all true— exactly as it was written down in the great book. Hadn't Gil Blas even met on his travels clans of the wandering Irish? 'An altercation never comes amiss to them. Such gestures! Such grimaces! Such contortions! Our eyes sparkling and our mouths foaming. Those who did not take us for what we affected to be, philosophers, must have set us down for madmen.'

Years afterwards, when living in Brussels, Charles Lever read Gil Blas. It influenced his work to the point of his taking poor Con Cregan from Kinnegad in Ireland, sending him over the sea to the New World, calling him the Irish Gil Blas, bringing him back to Spain and Italy, making him rich as Le Sage had made Gil Blas rich.[2] Dr. Maginn even said that Tom Burke and Harry Lorrequer and Charles O'Malley with their over-developed Ego resembled Gil Blas. But mere egotism was not enough. Mere travel over seas and continents was not enough. Merely getting rich was not enough. There was no moment when Lever's comedy gestured its way into the soul, as Le Sage's comedy did, as Carleton's comedy did. Gil Blas would have understood immediately had he lived late enough

[1] 'Barney Bradley's Resurrections.'
[2] *The Adventures of Con Cregan: The Irish Gil Blas*, by Charles Lever.

to see Dr. McClaret, the minister,[1] under the influence of the gentle passion, wearing tight inexpressibles and silk stockings, exchanging his shovel hat for a *chapeau*, even offering to learn to dance. A waltz, said Dr. McClaret, was a dance 'not disagreeable in certain cases . . . in which the gentleman puts his arm around the lady's waist—ahem!—round the lady's person, and they commence twirling around with considerable rapidity. Where the emotions are pure and good, and in any degree reciprocal, that appears to me a rather agreeable gyration; the emotion, besides, is philosophical and planetary.'

Somewhere beyond death Smollett and Le Sage must have laughed together, knowing one of their brothers.

For the book borrowed from the packman had gone directly to the soul of William Carleton. The world was before him and the world was picaresque. He could be one of those lunatic, philosophical, Irish wanderers. At eleven o'clock one morning he set off and walked twenty-five miles, passing by a few miles the town of Castleblayney. The wandering fellow from Santillane went beckoning before him. It was the first stage of his journey eastwards to the sea.

[1] *The Squanders of Castle Squander.*

FOUR

GIL BLAS was never able to forget what his people back in Santillane and Oviedo might think of his successes or failures. William Carleton with his back to the valley and his face to the world was trying desperately to convince himself that he had no home, no family, no people. Somewhere near Castleblayney he enjoyed the hospitality of a widow who came from the townland next to the townland in which his sister lived; and, through her kindness, he spent his first homeless night sleeping comfortably in a bed and a shooting-lodge that belonged to Lord Blayney. He told his hostess that he was going on the world, that nothing on God's earth would induce him to return to his people, that he hadn't a copper penny in his pocket. She opened up a mahogany chest-of-drawers, counted into his hand twenty-four tenpenny bits, and, heavier and richer, he took the road towards Carrickmacross, his back still to the valley and his people, losing friends and finding friends, until that proud day when he realised that he had found for ever the people of Ireland.

'I found them,' he wrote, 'a class unknown in literature, unknown by their own landlords, and unknown by those in whose hands much of their destiny was placed. If I became the historian of their habits and manners, their feelings, their prejudices, their superstitions and their crimes; if I have attempted to delineate their moral, religious and physical state, it was because I saw no person willing to undertake a task which surely must be looked upon as an important one. . . . I was anxious that those who ought, but did not, understand their character, should know them, not merely for selfish purposes, but that they should teach them to know themselves and appreciate their rights, both moral and civil, as rational men, who owe obedience to law, without the necessity of being slave either to priest or landlord. . . .[1]

He was leaving his people and going towards his people, coming out of one Irish valley to discover the secret of every Irish valley, to write his record of the joys and the desolation of the Irish. Always the writing of that record, at its best and most vivid and most colourful moments, involved a certain return to the boy lost for ever in the Ulster valley that the young man abandoned for ever when he went recklessly on the world. He said that something always drew him back to the scenes of his youth, to his native hills and glens, to the mountains and lakes and the precipices that turned his memory into 'one dreamy landscape, chequered by the clouds and sunshine of joy and tears.' The mountains remained unchanged, made

---

[1] Introduction to *Tales of Ireland* (Curry, Dublin, 1834).

always the same appeal to the returning heart. The river that ran twisting through the hazel glen could never hurt him as the world could hurt him. The low hill splendid with yellow broom was 'guiltless of a crime against the boy who sported and was joyful on it.'[1] For even Gil Blas who mastered the world knew that the world was a dangerous, wicked place; otherise he would never have written down the words spoken to him by the Duke of Lerma: 'You have escaped from the snares of this wicked world more by luck than management: it is wonderful that bad example should not have corrupted you irreparably. There are many men of strict virtue and exemplary piety, who would have turned out the greatest rogues in existence, if their destinies had exposed them to but half your trials.' Master Gil Blas was one of the lucky ones.

Near the parish of Killaney, in County Louth, William Carleton walked suddenly into a terrible townland of death, where decaying bodies swung on roadside gallows, poisoning the wind and the sun and the pure air, making the whole earth not only a wicked place, but the abode of hideous and unintelligible evil. He was then living with or living on his former school-fellow, Edward McArdle, who was parish priest of Killaney, who hadn't a book in his possession except his prayer-book, who couldn't provide his guest with anything to read. So the guest killed his time walking out over the autumn roads, filling his healthy lungs with the crisp air blowing over the flat land of Louth. At a cross-roads in a village he suddenly came upon a gallows, a few idle soldiers guarding the frightful thing and gossiping casually, and, in the 'slight but agreeable breeze . . . something like a tar-sack swinging backwards and forwards.' Long ropes of slime shone in the light and dangled from the bottom of the thing that swung in the air. In the pitched sack, the sergeant told him, was the body of a man called Paddy Devaun.

At that time Carleton had read only three newspapers. It was thirty years or so before a group of young men with new ideas for a new world made *The Nation* the first really popular newspaper that Ireland had known; and what newspapers there were, apparently penetrated very infrequently into the Clogher valley. But news had other ways of travelling, and Carleton's surprise on seeing that horrible, pestiferous thing really calls for more explanation than he ever gave. It is not a long journey from Killaney in Louth to Clogher in Tyrone, and even if he had not heard previously the terrible story of Wildgoose Lodge, it was nothing unique in a country where men were bitterly discontented about rent and tithes, where men really knew slavery and oppression and the black neighbourhood of perpetually threatening hunger, where men hated each other

[1] *Barney Brady's Goose, The Hedge School, The Three Tasks and other Irish tales* (Duffy, 1769).

because of differing creeds. That wicked rivalry of creeds, the sufferings of the majority at the hands of a rabid, government-supported minority had already touched his home and his people vividly enough to be remembered. But his first realisation of the misery of the land he walked in and the people to whom he belonged seems to have come to him suddenly at the foot of a gibbet in a village in Louth. Within ten miles radius of the village the horror was repeated again and again. On more than one walk he passed four swinging, guarded bodies, set up as terrible signs near the homes to which the unfortunate had belonged. Altogether there were twenty-four dead bodies hanging from gallows in that district and, in the warmth of an unusual Autumn, the bodies went the way of all flesh, the pitch melted, the sacks burst and the mixture of pitch and putrefaction trailed in slimy ropes right down to the ground. Women fainted at the sight. The flies gathered and fed and went away in buzzing swarms, and the people of Louth let the fruit lie rotting in the apple-orchards. Within a hundred yards of the gibbet on which Paddy Devaun was hanging, his mother walked in and out of her own door, busied herself about ordinary household duties, looked up now and again at the hideous thing and said: 'God be merciful to the soul of my poor marthyr.'

From one point of view Paddy Devaun was a martyr. From another point of view he was a murderer. The truth was somewhere between the two points of view. Not that there was any doubt about the murder. A family by the name of Lynch had lived, apparently quietly and inoffensively, in Wildgoose Lodge, refusing steadily to take part with their neighbours in the activities of the local Ribbon-men. 'The members of that accursed Ribbon Society,' wrote Carleton years afterwards,[1] 'instead of confining themselves to these objects for which it seems to have been originally designed— a union of Irishmen against their Protestant enemies, and the penal enactments which oppressed them at the time—departed from their original object, and employed its murderous machinery not against its open and common enemy, but in the following up of private and personal feuds, and enmities amongst themselves.' A natural end for the secret and violent thing in a land without order and without justice.

One night a mob smashed in the door of Wildgoose Lodge, battered and bruised the Lynch family with an outrageous amount of thoroughness. At Dundalk Assizes, on evidence given by the Lynch people, two of their unwelcome visitors were transported, and Paddy Devaun who, as parish-schoolmaster and parish-clerk was above suspicion, summoned a meeting in the parish chapel where every day he taught his school. On the altar of God vengeance

[1] O'Donoghue, vol. i.

was sworn; and, remembering the stories he heard then in Killaney, Carleton, the writer, was able to add the necessary amount of imaginative gloom and artistic horror.[1] He had seen only the decaying, rotten body of Paddy Devaun swinging on the gallows; but in imagination he heard the voice of Paddy Devaun swearing on God's book and on God's altar to do the deed that he and his associates had met to plan. He saw Paddy Devaun strike the book with his open hand, saw the candle that burned on the altar suddenly extinguished in a rush of wind, heard the oath of revenge echoed back from fifty places in the chapel. In Killaney he had heard stories of the burning and murder that happened at Wildgoose Lodge, and in his mind he saw the pyramid of flame rising into the sky as the last victim went back screaming; and the hills and the air and the floods then high in the flat land were like molten copper with the red reflection.

He was only passing through Killaney. He did not know where exactly he was going, where his next halt would be. He did not know that the road ahead would lead him to the day when he would sit down seriously to advise his people against parties and factions and agitations, against Ribbonism and Orangeism, against everything that had in it the horror of hate. What exactly would his serious advice have meant to that old woman crossing and recrossing her own threshold, looking up now and again to see, high against heaven, the body of her son? For she knew only that in pain she had given him life, that he had lived to clerk for the priest and to teach the children, that for some reason she could not fathom he had lost the life she gave him on the high gallows, in ignominy and pain. It was a sorrowful, foolish land; so sorrowful and foolish that the poets had seen it as an old bent woman perpetually mourning the death of her sons.

There was nothing in all the pages of Le Sage to parallel that journey between the gallows; but, all other things being equal, Gil Blas would have been at home in the house where Carleton made his next halt as tutor to the children of a strong farmer called Pierce Murphy. Murphy's farmyard was the largest Carleton had ever seen; his hogyard, his cattle, his general stock talked splendidly of wealth. It was all very impressive; and it remained in the memory until the story of Fardorougha, the miser, was written, and the wealth of Bodagh Buie O'Brien faithfully described. Murphy's temper was the worst in the world. The sight of a trespassing dog sent him into furies and murderous movements with a gun; and on behalf of a setter dog, the property of No-Popery Sir Harcourt Lees, the tutor had his first quarrel with the farmer. The last quarrel

[1] 'Wildgoose Lodge' (*Traits and Storie*).

ended with the tutor flattening the strong farmer on the grass-plot three yards from his own front door, and travelling on to Dundalk where his cousin Keenan was then in charge of his own classical school. By good, or bad luck he managed a lift with the driver of a hearse who raced towards Dundalk at a pace that would have been creditable in 'the chariot races of the Romans.'

On the speeding hearse the ex-tutor carried with him a few pleasant memories that remained in spite of Murphy's choler and the neighbouring shadow of the gallows. If Paddy Devaun came to a terrible end at the cross-roads of Corcreagh, life still continued for Peter Byrne and his three brothers who kept a tavern at that very place, for Gaynor the piper whose pipes didn't appear worth half a crown but whose playing silenced every sound, quieted every tongue, opened every ear, carried every spirit away 'by the incredible and unparalleled charm of his melody.' To the music of those pipes the tutor danced the Jig Polthogue and Miss Macleod's Reel with the handsomest girl in the room, danced with a knowledge of the dances that later amazed the learned Petrie when he was digging backwards through Ireland's social antiquities, danced so as to amaze there and then the people of the place astounded to discover the supple, muscular, rhythmical powers of a young gentleman who was also master of the seven languages. He was, he said, 'urged forward by an unequivocal impulse of vanity'; yet it is just in such braggadocio moments that he suddenly stands symbolically for the whole Irish people, dancing merrily over the grave and under the gallows, riding in a hearse and going at a gallop from a discarded but vividly-remembered past into an unknown future.

Cousin Keenan was not enthusiastic. The man's health was failing and he could whip up no welcome for the relation who came to him riding uproariously in the carriage of death. Looking with unkind moodiness at Cousin William he said: 'You came like a bird of evil omen to pay your visit to me. I suppose you thought there was something significant and prophetic of my state of health in the vehicle you pitched upon to perform your journey.' It was superstitious. It was also 'cruel and unchristian,' for what it meant in practice was that Cousin Keenan who owned a school had no employment for Cousin William who considered himself a teacher, who was also 'without a coin from His Majesty's Mint' in his possession. He went southwards along the coast towards Dublin, reached Drogheda on the Boyne, found lodgings with a landlady who surpassed all termagants 'in or out of hell.' That was a favourite phrase of his. Her mouth was thin and unfeeling. Her eyes were sharp and piercing and actually emitted fire. She seemed perpetually in a fury, and the penniless master of seven languages confessed

41

to himself that he was anything but at ease. Before he went to bed she sequestrated the scholar's shirt in case he should happen also to be a swindler and, although he slept soundly, he left her house shirtless and walked down by the broad Boyne bitterly cursing Gil Blas and blaming his own gullibility. To sailors on a ship in the river he sold a handkerchief for two shillings, remembered that he had once been initiated into the mysteries of Ribbonism, tapped the tip of his nose with his middle-finger, had answering taps from four sailors, and left the quayside with eight shillings and sixpence and his handkerchief generously returned to him. Even Ribbonism had its uses.

From Drogheda he went deeper into County Louth to Ardee, to discover a jolly fellow and a happy man whose real name was Peter Murray but who loved only those who knew him as the 'Ardee dog.' Maybe on the road back to Dundalk he thought the thoughts that he afterwards wrote down: 'God help us! How many admirable and original characters are there in life of whom the world neither has nor knows anything, men whom to examine would present a profound and interesting study to him who wishes to become thoroughly acquainted with human nature. They pass away, however, like the phantoms of a dream, and leave no memory or impression behind them. *Qui caveat sano vate!*'[1]

The crazy road that he followed on foot was showing him sad men and happy men, possibly a very large proportion of hungry men, for, in 1817, the hunger that followed the people like a shadow had deepened into famine. Thirty years later, under the still deeper shadow of a more horrible famine, he wrote *The Black Prophet*, dedicated it to an English Prime Minister, filled its pages with the terrible things he had seen in 1817. His people were threatened with a more total oblivion than anything that could result from the mere passing of time and the failing memory of man. The sad and the happy and the hungry could go down forgotten into bottomless darkness. But a penniless young fellow following a road as planless as his whole life was to put out his hand and call the doomed millions back from the blackness that was so much less even than the chaos and confusion of their perilous lives. He was roaming the country, talking to men and women, merely a man among the other men; but the road was twisting forward to his destiny, to the writing of words that would preserve forever the memory of a people.

He went to a place called the Fane valley, to a man called Fitzgerald, whose son grew up to be an antiquarian and an author;

[1] O'Donoghue, vol. i, p. 165.

and while Fitzgerald the father was a perfect gentleman he had already engaged a schoolmaster, and Carleton heard for the first time that there was a Society in Kildare Street in Dublin that taught fellows to be schoolmasters. Above the polite words of Fitzgerald of Fane Valley he must have heard the high mockery of the laughter of Mat Kavanagh of Findramore, for 'it was a poor proof of qualification for such an office, that it was found necessary to teach any man his duties.' So the untaught and unemployed schoolmaster footed it back to Dundalk, wrote a final appeal to Cousin Keenan who, still thinking of morbid and macabre things and of ominous hearses, wrote back to say that Cousin William might find himself a job with some undertaker. William was hurt. He was also puzzled by the word 'undertaker' which he had never heard before. He moved about erratically from house to house, finding kindness and hospitality among the people of Dundalk, discovering also in himself a talent for transmogrifying and changing the classical stories, for improvising endlessly on ancient themes. He was his father's son; and if stories were all he had to offer in return for food, bedding and good cheer, he was, in that, reaching back into the past and touching on an ancient tradition. He was also reaching forward into his own future, finding, unknown to himself, a door into his own soul and a touch or a charm that would preserve for ever his own memories.

A schoolmaster met by chance one day advised him onwards to the town of Navan in the rich lands of Meath. There was a 'celebrated Catholic boarding-school' there, and, maybe, an opening for an usher, but, although he wrote a letter to the 'pious and amiable Bishop of Meath, the Right Rev. Doctor Plunket' and although the Bishop forwarded the letter to the Reverend Dr. O'Reilly who ruled the school, his journey and his petition had no result, beyond burning his soul with a desire to pull Dr. O'Reilly's nose. The desire was smothered in respect for the clerical state and the clerical cloth.

But in Navan he met a man called Gaynor, a pious man, a hospitable man, a learned tailor, even if he was no classical scholar; and in a house by a lake in that green quiet country he picked up and read for the first time the story that honest Thady Quirk had told of the decline and fall of the house of Rackrent. Faraway in Russia Ivan Turgenev heard the fading, lamenting voice of Thady, living and dying 'loyal to the family,' and wondered could he do for the wide plains of his own land what the precise, word-perfect spirit of Maria Edgeworth was doing for that desolate western island. Walter Scott heard the voice above the rattle of old stories of the Border, the horse-hooves of troopers, the slither of swords and the clash of armoured men meeting in battle. In Scott the voice of Thady inspired a quiet, less colourful mood with moments of steady contemplation showing him the souls of his own people.

43

By the lake in Meath wandering, workless William Carleton thought the story of *Castle Rackrent* 'inimitable,' and, as far as he himself was concerned, the word was well chosen. He was as far separated from that precision in word and idea as he was from Scott's great imaginative power for revivifying and recolouring the past, as they all were from the eastern world of Turgenev.

About that time, at Edgeworthstown over in Longford and not a million miles from Navan, the father of Maria Edgeworth, trusting that the British public would sympathise with what a father felt for his daughter's literary success, defiantly wrote his last preface,[1] delivered his last advice, and died. Public critics, as he called them, had found fault with him for perpetually prefacing his daughter's books. Public critics had even found fault with those books; and Miss Edgeworth, through her father, took the opportunity of that preface to thank the critics for the candid and lenient manner in which her errors had been pointed out. The wind would blow for many days across Longford and across Meath before one more candid and lenient critic would point out that when Miss Edgeworth fell before fashion and wrote her essay on Irish bulls she wrote an essay 'upon that which does not, and never did exist.' She should have known that 'where the English *is* vernacular in Ireland, it is spoken with far more purity and grammatical precision than is to be heard beyond the Channel.' But Miss Edgeworth had been one of the three women who had done much 'in setting right the character of Ireland and her people, whilst exhibiting at the same time the manifestations of high genius.' She had surpassed both Lady Morgan and Mrs. Hall in endowing 'her female creations' with 'a touching charm, blending the graceful and the pensive, which reminds us of a very general but peculiar type of Irish beauty, where the lineaments of the face combine at once both the melancholy and the mirthful in such a manner that their harmony constitutes the unchangeable but ever-varying tenderness of the expression.'[2]

Very candid and very lenient; the critic remembering possibly that day by the lake at Navan, the delight and enchantment of discovering a new mind, a new user of words. Forty years later Miss Edgeworth, having discovered in the meantime the Irish people as Carleton knew them, more intimately than she herself had ever seen them, wrote to add her name to the list of notables supporting Carleton in his appeal for a pension. She wrote down her admiration for his talents, her esteem for his works that gave 'with such

---

[1] Preface to the first edition of *Harrington, a Tale* and *Ormond, a Tale,* in three vols., by Maria Edgeworth. London: Printed for R. Hunter, successor to Mr. Johnson, 72 St. Paul's Churchyard, 1870.

[2] Longer Introduction to the *Traits and Stories*

masterly strokes and in such strong and vivid colours the picture of our country's manners, her virtues, and her vices, without ministering to party prejudices or exciting dangerous passions, to produce authorship effect or to win temporary applause.'[1] It was praise spoken very much in the style of old Edgeworth the writer of prefaces whose prefacing and marrying ended back in the days when William Carleton was without a reputation or a red penny or a roof over his head. A friend once equally condemned Carleton and Maria Edgeworth for the over-demonstrative titles: *The Squanders of Castle Squander* and *Castlerent*; going on to write that Miss Edgeworth's tales were flat,[2] with no heart-stirring love-making, with none of the vitality of actual life in Ireland. William Carleton who knew a good deal about that vitality and that love-making didn't think so; but whispering 'inimitable' he ended the story and moved southwards from Navan into the county of Kildare. For Gaynor, the tailor, had gone on business to Mullingar, leaving Carleton lacking congenial company.

He was going to Maynooth not as a scholar, not even as Denis O'Shaughnessy, but as a young man seeing the sights: places and people and high buildings. Even more than he had once wanted to see Lough Derg, he now wanted to see Maynooth. At Kilcock, the son of the man he lodged with for a night advised him that, since he was in the neighbourhood, he could do no better than see Clongowes College and the Jesuit fathers. In 'a letter written at the very top of his skill' he offered his services to fill a vacancy that unfortunately did not exist, but six or seven of the fathers interviewed him in a large room where they whispered occasionally in the distant corners. He dined in solitary state and was quietly presented with an envelope containing fifteen shillings and, although he had failed in his attempt to bring into alliance the educational ideas of Mat Kavanagh and St. Ignatius, he was, half-a-century afterwards, remembering his hosts as reverend and learned fathers.

In Maynooth the Duke of Leinster was celebrating his recent marriage by adding additional buildings to his castle. The 'beggarly-looking and contemptible village' was crowded with workmen. The house in which the wanderer found lodgings was crowded with workmen and cursed with a landlord who spent most of his time ill-treating his own children, until the new lodger restored the balance of justice by beating the landlord in a battle that lasted for twenty terrible minutes, leaving him with eyes 'bunged up' and face disfigured, kicking him out of his own house into the street because the chastised papa refused, naturally enough, to show his appreciation,

[1] O'Donoghue, vol. ii. [2] O'Donoghue, vol. ii.

good humour and Christianity, by laughing as he was told to laugh. Afterwards he sat down and wrote a note to the Rev. Paul O'Brien, professor of Irish in the college, and the author of an Irish grammar, asking permission to see the buildings and the surrounding grounds, and Father Paul who was a 'droll man and a humorist' responded to the letter and personally showed the strange visitor the sights.

At school with him back in the Clogher Valley there had been a poor scholar, a lad called John Quin who came from somewhere near Enniskillen, a poor scholar in every imaginable way. It was all part of the world's ironic way of doing things that, standing at the gate of the college, William Carleton should see Jonh Quin, now a student for the priesthood but not wishing to be recognised, anxious obviously to forget the days of poverty and poor scholarship. The snobbery implied, prejudiced the easily-prejudiced visitor against the body of the students of Saint Patrick's, making them less in his memory than Judy Byrne who sold fruit to the college, who was 'a woman by mistake.' Her huge body wore, outside the conventional female coverings, a man's short outside-coat. On her head she had a man's hat. Her tongue was cool, brazen and uncontrolled. Her lodgings in the centre of the town were comfortable, and fragrant with stored fruit. She boasted that in days of red rebellion she had been a United Irishman. She called the clerics and learned professors by their surnames and, meeting the Duke of Leinster, bellowed manfully: 'Well, Fitzgerald, how long are you married now?' The regulator of the college clocks was 'the celebrated Irish giant, Big Magee' who had been exhibited all over the world, who confided in Carleton that, in the intervals of the occupation for which he claimed he had been brought to Maynooth, he had almost discovered the secret of perpetual motion.

From Maynooth he went down the calm Liffey valley country, wondering, maybe, what would have happened to Denis O'Shaughnessy had he stayed in Maynooth, or what would have happened to himself had he braved at Granard the fury of the bull that ran and roared through his homesick dream. Would he have stood by the college gate shiveringly ashamed of his past and his poverty and his own people? Would the little trace of threadbare snobbery and barren pride that was actually in him have infected him, blood and bone? He slept a night in Celbridge. He was an unsuccessful hedge-schoolmaster at Newcastle in County Dublin. Idle speculation, anyhow, didn't matter any longer. Denis O'Shaughnessy, the mortal, was dead. Denis O'Shaughnessy, the immortal, was not yet born; and in the travail and torture that preceded his birth William Carleton, the idle boy, the dancer and leaper and weight-thrower, the lover of story and music and song, the lover of round hills and

46

green fields and quiet valleys, the lover of his own people, was to die a dozen, different deaths.

It was all before him, down the valley in Dublin, a city full of people, and in cities men buried dreams and uncovered wisdom. Maybe, he said, like Gil Blas, I may after struggles and adventures find at last a calm and safe harbour. So he walked down the great southern road and in James's Street the houses of the proud, shabby city cast their shadows over his path. He was walking in a land of shadows.

FIVE

Wʜᴇɴ Tom McMahon came back to Ahadarra[1] from the big city of Dublin the poteen bottle was left uncorked on the dresser and the neighbours crowded in to hear the news. Jemmy Kelly and Paddy Mullin ran in, Paddy hatless and coatless where he had been digging in his garden. They asked him question after question about the city and the wonders of the city, about the murders and robberies committed upon travellers, about the kidnapping of strangers from the country, about the Lord Lieutenant's Castle with its three hundred and sixty-four windows. Around the hearth in Ahadarra they talked of Dublin as if it were as wonderful to them and as far away as Samarcand or the remote cities of Cathay.

Carleton heard the neighbours talk that way in Towney or Prillisk or Springtown when a traveller returning across Meath and Monaghan sat down to tell of wonderful things he had seen and strange things that had happened. His own pictures of the city that he walked into in the year 1818 are unromantic enough, sombre and shadowed, but burning with a red light of life like a fire in a darkened cellar.

Tom McMahon might have eaten his meals during his stay in Dublin in the eating-house in Little Mary Street where so much villainy was debated in the story of 'The Black Baronet.' A lap of beef hung from an iron hook on the doorpost, black with flies in summer, capable of leaving on your coat a healthy streak of 'something between grease and tallow.' Inside, the provincial visitor was represented by two or three large County Meath farmers with immense frieze jackets, corduroy knee-breeches, thick woollen stockings and heavy-soled shoes; the city-worker appeared in a few meagre-looking scrivener's clerks rather out-at-elbows. Or moving along the streets towards the Marshalsea debtors' prison Tom's innocent eyes might have seen but not understood the winks and leers of a certain class of female who would feel 'the influence of religion and moral principle just as soon as a sound cork would absorb water.' Randy O'Rollick saw them, when he went to visit Squire Squanders in captivity, passing in and out of the Marshalsea, transacting business for the prisoners. There were orange girls, oyster wenches, flying confectioners with the readiest smile for the man of most rakish appearance.

But Tom and Randy, and William Carleton must have felt themselves separated by vague yet real enough barriers from the odd

---

[1] *The Emigrants of Ahadarra.*

life of the streets and the houses. In an old ballad the lad arriving in Dublin to 'try for a situation' was blessed in the possession of a sublime adaptability that is given to few men. He was a roving, sporting blade who placed his chief delight in courting the girls and who was known as the Jack-of-all-Trades. He was ready for anything; and all he knew about Dublin was that 'it was the pride of all the nation.'

> *'On George's Quay,'* he sang, *'I first began, where I became a*
> *porter;*
> *Me and my master soon fell out which cut my acquaintance shorter.*
> *In Sackville Street a pastrycook; in James's Street a baker;*
> *In Cook Street I did coffins make; in Eustace Street a pr'acher.*
>
> *In College Green I banker was; in Smithfield Square a drover;*
> *In Britain Street a waiter; in George's Street a glover.*
> *On Ormond Quay I sold old books; in King Street was a nailer;*
> *In Townsend Street a carpenter, and in Ringsend a sailor.'*

William Carleton had before him all those streets and all those choices of profession. But the young man who had rejected the joys of stone-cutting and talking the classics with Lanty Doain was unlikely to be drawn away into less dignified occupations in the lanes of Dublin. Some higher destiny was still before him. What it was or where it was he did not know. It was scarcely in houses like the seaside villa called Tusculum where Mrs. Raffarty, the merchant's wife, entertained Lord Colambre and her own high pretensions in a drawing-room 'fine with bad pictures and gaudy gildings,' with the windows all shut and the company playing cards.[1] For even the world of Lord Colambre, the son of the absentee landlord, was tortured in a time of transition that began when the members of the College Green parliament took their bribes and voted for the Union.

Walking into James's Street, jingling a few pennies in his pocket, William Carleton knew little enough about the passing of the Union, the politics of Lord Castlereagh, the perilous grandeur of the merchant's wife, the isolated and exceptional patriotism of Lord Colambre, who decided suddenly to return to Ireland and work for the good of the people who lived on his land. He was a raw fellow from the country, as raw as Paul the Shot[2] when a practical joker sent him all the way to Dublin to purchase a 'piano-forty' and, incidentally, to assault a Protestant bishop in the hall of his own Georgian house. Carleton knew only that with the purse he possessed it would be foolish to think of penetrating further than the suburbs,

[1] 'The Absentee.'
[2] 'Alley Sheridan or The Runaway Match.'

49

into the busy streets and stately squares of the central city. So he turned sideways down a lane and found lodgings. Later he discovered that the place was called Dirty Lane. He thought that ominous. He had also his own little superstitions about the number of the house, which was forty-eight.

Those first years of life in Dublin must have given him for his own forever the secret of the streets of Dublin as Dickens was given in his boyhood the secret of the incredible world that is the streets of London. But Dickens was at home in London, walking familiar pavements, surrounded by familiar houses, inhaling the air of London as the sustaining power of his whole body and soul. Carleton was never at home in Dublin. In a certain sense no man of the native Irish could then have been completely at home in Dublin for in Dublin all the cross-purposes and perplexed wastages of the chaotic country were made increasingly obvious. It was a capital and it was not a capital. It had the passing attentions of an aristocracy that was not properly an aristocracy; for the lands of the aristocrats were in Ireland but their hearts were in London, and Dublin filled some middle world of nothingness between the pleasures of London and the rack-rented, declining Irish estates. It had a growing and gradually stabilising merchant class, with a Catholic element feeling haltingly about for shreds and tatters of the municipal and political power that decades of legislation hostile to Catholics had left them lacking. All this passed for a time over his head like the whirring flight of a flock of birds. He was down, deep down in small rooms and narrow streets living with the poor, and the shiftless vagrants, and the destitute, and the hard men who worked with their hands. He never wrote a great story about those people as he wrote great stories about the people who filled the lanes, the fields, the cabins, the farmhouses, the places of prayer and the places of jollification in the days of his youth. One reason was that the Irish people lived or existed out in country places. The city was an anomaly. Brick walls and paved streets in such puzzling, complicated quantities had all the oddity of an eruption or a fantastic growth. One hundred years had to pass before an Irish novelist told the story of the streets of Dublin, following the pattern used by Homer when he sent his hero wandering from the streets of Troy. The novel in question was published in Paris, and interested and enlightened and scandalised most of the cities of the western world.

But then James Joyce had been at home in Dublin, happy and unhappy in Dublin. Dublin was in his bones. In Paris or in Trieste he sat down to write, and remembered Dublin. William Carleton did his writing where Joyce had left his heart. But he looked back across flat land to the valley where the grass was more green and the sunshine more golden than anywhere else in the wide world. He saw also a thousand valleys and a thousand hill-slopes, bare places on mountains, flat land along rivers, stony places by the sea. Everywhere he saw his people, eight millions of them on one small island. Above them the sky was blackening with the darkness of doom.

Fifty years afterwards in one of the most interesting passages of his unfinished autobiography he wrote down one after another the things Dublin did to him when he walked in, raw and inexperienced, from the countryside that was Ireland.

In Dirty Lane his first Dublin landlord was a quiet, good-natured, easily-imposed-upon man with a handsome young wife whose three mysterious brothers lived practically at free quarters on her husband. The three men ran a Punch and Judy Show in Moore Street. The good-natured man brought Carleton to see Punch and Judy, telling him in the intervals between 'legerdemain tricks' that threw the lodger into 'convulsions of laughter,' that the handsome wife had once been part of the Punch and Judy business, that he had to bribe the brothers into consenting to the marriage. Knowing as little of the world as he possessed of the world's property the lodger believed what the gulled landlord told him. Then that lack of worldly possessions, his inability to pay his bills and to stand treat to the three showmen, sent him across the lane to new lodgings, down steps into a spacious cellar, revisited in thought in later years when he read *The Jolly Beggars*, recalled to his mind by certain tense and embarrassing moments in Dante's *Inferno*. In that cellar in Dirty Lane he saw for the first time the red centre of his country's degraded beggary, and his bred-in-the-bone rural respectability writhed in horror. There had been beggars in his native valley, beggars on the roads he had tramped on his way to Dublin. But that was beggary with a difference, with a certain dignity, with a link with a lost way of life in which the wandering poor had a certain high mystical significance. There had been the slightly suspicious piety of the voteen, the Shakespearean stature of the fool. Samuel Lover wrote that in Ireland 'the fool, or natural, or innocent, as represented in the stories of the Irish peasantry, is very much the fool that Shakespeare occasionally embodies; and, even in the present day, many a witticism and sarcasm, given birth to by these mendicant Touchstones, would be treasured in the memory of our *beau monde*, under the different heads of brilliant or biting, had they been uttered by a Bushe or a Plunket.'[1]

Through Carleton's memory ran the great figures of Tom Steeple,

[1] *Legends and Stories of Ireland.*

of Raymond-a-hattha, and even Art the fool who was less than the others because he was merely cunning—all these in good time to be given lasting life as essential, unforgettable parts of the stories of Willy Reilly, of Valentine McClutchy, of philandering Phelim O'Toole. He saw as in a vision the long, powerful body of Raymond ' as wild and untamed as the barren waste on which he made his appearance.'[1] Adding to his monstrous height he wore three hats one on top of the other, a long surtout, buttoned closely and reaching to his heels. He wore neither boot nor shoe but cased his feet in a pair of tight leather buskins, and always on his left hand a glove but never any on his right. His whole appearance was like that of 'a new and well-proportioned house which has never been occupied, everything seemed externally regular and perfect, whilst it was evident by its still and lonely character . . . that it was void and without an inhabitant.' Tom Steele was not a tall fool, but, imbedded somewhere in his poor quagmire of a mind, was the delusion that he was taller than all other men, as tall in fact as a towering steeple; in that fancy of madness there was a certain significance. For Carleton really saw Tom and Raymond as tall men, standing high above the legions of destitute and homeless. They were poorer than the poorest, for the world they walked on was in ways as meaningless as a crazy pavement or a patchwork quilt. But from the deepest deeps of misery they stood symbolically erect, speaking wit and wisdom, doing good deeds out of the warm overflowing of generous hearts, showing the thousand ways in which that western island of beggary could be as rich as the fabulous East.

Going down the steps to the cellar in Dirty Lane he lost for the moment that vision. On shakedowns of straw with sheets of rag, men and women in various degrees of drink lay asleep. By the light of a red fire he saw the lame, the blind, the dumb, broken and diseased people. He saw also those who, during the day and for business purposes, had assumed all the infirmities of the flesh. Crutches, wooden legs, artificial cancers, scrofulous necks, artificial wens, sore legs, dangled on the dirty walls. Those who were still awake sang and chatted and shouted slang, and the lad from the green country felt for the first time the creeping touch of a leprous obscenity. They spoke him civilly, offered him a seat, and a few young, vagabondish pick-pockets approached him in friendly fashion, and he spoke to them with the indifferent ease of the man who had paid twopence for his bed and had exactly one penny left in his pocket. Once again there was nothing like it in Gil Blas; there was nothing like it on the roads where the beggars and voteens went, on the hills the pilgrims crossed walking to the holy island, in the

1 'Valentine McClutchy.'

airy elevation where the minds of Raymond of the Hats and Tom Steeple were isolated from the woes of men. But when the red fire died in the cellar and he lay listening to the uneasy moving of those wretches in their sleep, it is just possible that a cold wind may have come whispering down the steps from Dirty Lane, telling of horror in the cabins and green fields, of putridity in potato-furrows and a stench rising from the cultivated land, of a whole people dying in a rottenness that shivered fearfully on the edge of the obscene.

He was two years in Dublin when he married a wife. They were not his poorest years. He had no possessions and his wealth could almost always be counted in pennies, but neither had he any responsibilities. They were homeless years, and he was the home-loving type of man who felt with especial keenness the bitter lot of the homeless. They were aimless years, even for a man whose life lacked always the impulse and aim of continued purpose. He walked the streets of Dublin vaguely hoping for employment somewhere at some time as a teacher, discovering that half the schools in Dublin were 'hedge-schools,' conducted up stairways and in shabby rooms by men who were illiterate and ignorant and not to be compared with the hedge-schoolmasters in country places. Urban degeneracy, the corruption that went with paved streets and endless brick walls, had tainted even the breed of Mat Kavanagh.

In Castle Street he saw his own name written large above the shop of a ladies' shoemaker, noted carefully the name of the street, returned later to appeal to the better instincts of his namesake. Across the counter he saw a handsome gentleman, thought by contrast of his own destitution and burst into tears. The shoemaker gave him five shillings and had in return something of immortality.

In lodgings in Moore Street he met a man called MacDonagh, a literary tailor perpetually writing the story of his own life but unable to spell or write a legible hand. So on Sundays in the summer Carleton and the tailor walked out into the country, sat down in the corner of a field, the tailor dictated and Carleton wrote. Or rather the tailor tried to dictate, for the choice and marshalling and steadying of ideas necessary in good dictation completely shattered the man's natural fluency of speech. One day Carleton suggested that the tongue-tied tailor should give only the bare facts, and 'with an easy spirit of fiction' he added and amplified and arranged. That night in the lodgings the tailor snapped his fingers and danced for joy, marvelling at the well-written fragment of his autobiography, and William Carleton, the writer, was born and had his first winy, intoxicating taste of public appreciation and patronage. It was the oddest of odd ways to begin writing. It was also a very ominous form of patronage. For the tailor who had promised, in place of wages, to pay his secretary's account with the landlady, went away one day and did not return.

In Mary's Lane he lodged with a Mrs. Carson, a widow, wonderful in the way of all widows, ostentatiously lavishing attentions on him until he was forced to move again, gallantly paying his bill this time. She had confided in him that she was going to a new house in Henry Street or Mary Street, that she had saved one hundred and forty pounds, that—with her brother's help—she would open a boarding establishment. She said: they tell me it's coining and nothing else. She said, also, that she didn't breakfast until the other lodgers went out, that Carleton and herself would then have the house to themselves, but that he shouldn't really take advantage of that circumstance to make love to her. He hadn't made love to her. He hadn't intended to make love to her. He felt 'a very uncomfortable sense of degradation at the notion of being tied to such a woman.'

In French Street he applied, a day too late, to a Protestant clergyman for a post as a classical teacher in the inevitably recurring classical school. But the kindly clergyman encouraged him to unburden his soul in the telling of his hopes and tribulations, treated him to his first drink of wine, secretly slipped three pounds into the lining of his hat, invited him to call again.

In Francis Street, south of the Liffey, he found a new home in a house that contained a circulating library, where he read from twelve to sixteen hours every day, wondering as he read about the morality of his landlady who was keeper of the library. For 'such a mass of obscenity and profligacy was (out of Holywell Street, the Jewish establishment in London) never put together.' He read the history of Mrs. Leeson otherwise known as the infamous Peg Plunkett. He read the history of the Chevalier de Faublas. He read the woeful adventures of the Irish Female Jockey Club 'a repertory of the antique scandal of the fashionable demireps of that day.'

Between Francis Street and Patrick Street was Plunket Street where Dublin bought and sold secondhand clothes. Searching there for a new suit, he was greeted with a shout of joy and recognition by the proprietor of one of the shops. He was the brother of Jemmy Donnelly who was also Jemmy McEvoy, the poor scholar; and the generous dealer in clothes insisted on dressing 'from top to toe, gratuitously' the man who was to immortalise his brother.

In Peter Street he looked for work in Mr. Kane's Classical Academy, discovered that Mr. Kane's black-dressed body was the lumpiest, most awkward, most ungainly body he had ever seen, that his face was the dullest, dreariest, reddest, ugliest of faces, that his legs were big enough for the carrier of a sedan chair, and his fists big enough for Tom Cribb, the pugilist. But his heart was a

Christian heart and his words were the words of a gentleman, and the recommendation he gave to William Carleton found him his first job in Dublin, as private tutor to the son of a man called Fox.

It was a shifting, changing life, as lacking in steady purpose and definite aim as the dancing of the Dublin Jack-of-all-Trades from one occupation to another. But even Master Jack was handling hard practical instruments, learning to buy and sell, learning to cheat and to avoid being cheated, learning casually the tricks and terminologies of a dozen trades. Carleton was, in his poverty, playing the gentleman in Dublin as he had played the gentleman in the Clogher valley. The sun might shine at night and the world turn backwards on its course, but those strong hands would never be stained by contact with common labour. He would burst into tears and accept five shillings from a namesake. He would gratefully discover in the lining of his hat the three pounds given by the charitable clergyman. He would accept a suit of clothes from the brother of the boy who had persevered, as Carleton had not persevered, on the poor scholar's path to Munster. There was no degradation in the charity that the poor scholar accepted from the people of the country. But there was something in that five shillings and three pounds and the gratuitous suit of clothes that weakened the backbone, preparing him for the day when he would accept a rather designing charity and betray part of himself and part of his people. His reading had not introduced him to the story of the poor Oxford student called Samuel Johnson who threw out of his window the badly-needed pair of boots offered in charity because, sir, a man should always stand in his own boots.

William Carleton mightn't even have understood that story. After all, he could ease his conscience with the words the gipsy woman spoke over him to his sister Mary, when they passed by the camp of the wanderers near the beautiful lough of Ballagh. She said he would never be a priest because he loved the girls too well, but he would go to Dublin and become a great man. She said nothing about great men wearing their own boots or even standing steadily on their own feet.

SIX

HE GAVE various reasons for changing his mind about becoming a priest, from the terror of the dream-bull to the exclusive salvation which he imagined was a Catholic doctrine. The reason given by the fortune-telling woman sounds as sensible as any. Denis O'Shaughnessy returned from Maynooth, and, in the words of his darling Susan Connor, took the kiss and spared the King's English. But loving the girls too well implied nothing that was not completely innocent. Carleton, the writer, had in his writings the conventional respect of the writers of his time for the image of the pure woman. With Madame Bovary the fashion swept round to feeling for the unfortunate woman, following, in some cases, the obvious truth that Blake had put into poetry about every harlot having once been a virgin, in other cases admiring, after Lorenzo Valla, misfortune and harlotry for their own sweet sakes. And Carleton the man had in his life nothing that in any way contradicted that worship of the fragile but unbroken, the incandescent gentility that was stronger than the world, the flesh and the devil.

His first love had been Mary Anne Dumont, daughter of the stately widow of the Frenchman lost in the Revolution. He was not then ten years of age and his professions of passion were confined, as they usually are at that age, to the blunt and imperfectly understood statement that he wanted to marry Mary Anne. It was scarcely of that affair he was thinking when he wrote about the way young Clinton felt for the chaste and slightly incredible Maria Brindsley.[1] Maria's image was, for Clinton, 'associated with that wonderful charm of delight and ecstasy which always characterises first love, but no other, for alas, it is the Eden of youth into which the heart can never enter a second time.' That statement on first love would have warmed the heart of Goethe wailing about the imperfection of every love except the first love, for love returning for the second or third time had become transient like all things that return. Goethe was in the way of knowing about such things, much more so than William Carleton in Dublin, than Billy Carleton in the Clogher Valley looking up suddenly on Easter morning at Mass and seeing the beauty of Anne Duffy, the daughter of the miller of Augher.

They were at Mass in the Forth. The congregation knelt in the open air on a circle of green grass about a hundred yards in diameter, and around the circle the ancient grass-grown ditch built in lost ages by a forgotten people. On the ditch on one side sat the young men,

---

[1] *The Double Prophecy* or *The Trials of the Heart.*

separated from but looking directly across at the young women; and around the altar were the young men and women whose voices were sweet enough to be heard in sacred song. Among them was 'one tall, elegant, and lady-like girl, whose voice was perfectly entrancing.' He heard her and saw her and was entranced. After Mass he followed her at a respectful distance, like a man hearing fairy music or a man walking in a dream, down the road to Augher as far as Ned McKeown's cross-roads where the men, gathered around the door of the shop, talked about the Peninsular War and hoped for the day when Bonaparte would be king of Ireland. Her father was there in the middle of them, a great cross-roads politician; and the lad listened to the father and lovingly eyed the daughter. She eyed back again with amused pleasure, filling his mind with an exquisite, idealised presence, sending him to the accepted solitary communing in the hazel-glen behind the house at Springtown. For three years and six months he followed her from Sunday Mass, to the corner of the side-street in Augher that led down to her father's mill. But he never spoke to her, never attempted to speak to her, and one autumn evening when his eldest brother said that the miller's daughter had married a man in the townland of Ballyscally, William slipped quietly out to the cold barn and cried for his broken dreams. He spoke to her years afterwards when he was a famous man, revisiting his native district. They exchanged commonplaces, and he said jokingly to her husband that Anne Duffy was the only woman he ever loved beyond the power of language to express. And the woman said before her husband that she had loved William Carleton as she had never loved another man, that it hadn't been their fate to become man and wife, that had William Carleton married Anne Duffy the world might never have heard of William Carleton, that anyway Anne Duffy was happily married in Ballyscally.

There was innocence in that story. There was also pathos and a little homely fun. He saw the fun detachedly when he described the method by which Paddy-Go-Easy made his love known to Nancy.[1] Paddy strode after her to Mass or market, wherever she went following her with 'an indescribable and oafish stare, that, to anyone who did not understand him, had more of felony than love in it.' The parish began to talk about Paddy. Biddy Brady, the match-maker advised him to make a bold push and ask her like a man instead of streeling after her like a constable trying to find out where she lived. But Paddy-Go-Easy like William Carleton went about the gentle business in his own odd way, succeeding where William failed because of his youth, possibly because there was no

[1] *Parra Sastha*, or *The History of Paddy-Go-Easy and his wife Nancy* (Duffy's Library of Ireland).

Biddy Brady to scheme and contrive his distant dreaming into active practical energy.

The women of his stories live always in the radiance of that homely, pathetic, good-humoured innocence, because of his own personal experience and the literary conventions of the time and the fact that he lived on an island where even today the respect for the virgin can be puzzling to visitors. The vision was not destroyed even by the horror drifting like a mist through the pages of *The Black Prophet*. The face of Mave Sullivan, the heroine of that story, is 'replete with an expression of innocence and youth' leaving on the beholder the 'conviction that she breathed of utter guilelessness and angelic purity.' and her smile could turn the hatred of hell into love. Cathleen Cavanagh in *The Emigrants of Ahadarra* was the other type of good woman, almost the biblical valiant woman, resolute, firm, immutable in her resolutions that were seldom hasty or unadvised but the result of rectitude and good sense, enthusiastically and rather sternly loving her religion, possessing high feelings of self-respect. Her type is not uncommon in Ireland. Going on in years they can develop the holy patience that he saw in Honor Donavan, the wife of Fardorougha the Miser; his own mother sitting for a large part of that portrait. But, naturally and artistically, he saw more in Cathleen Cavanagh than her moral strength. That good girl might have been something between flattered and annoyed if she could have read her creator's comment on her physical perfections: her 'voluptuous fullness of outline,' her exquisitely small foot, her 'finely swelling' leg, her full bust which 'literally glowed with light and warmth' and was 'moulded with inimitable proportion.' He saw all his own heroines with the eyes of first love, with the warm imagination of a boy burning for the idealised and the heroic. He saw them much as Willy Reilly saw for the first time the beauty of Helen Folliard, the Squire's daughter and the Cooleen Bawn. 'Such a blaze of beauty, such elegance of person, such tenderness and feeling as chastened the radiance of her countenance . . . such symmetry of form, such harmony of motion.' Very naturally the gallant Reilly was absorbed, entranced, struck with a sensation of wonder, surprise and agitation; his manly and intrepid heart being smitten duly began to palpitate.

Years after Flaubert, that mood of high admiration and ecstasy may seem a very naive and pitiful thing, but it had its meaning and its relation to life, it had its roots somewhere in a forgotten, buried chivalry. It could degenerate from praise of the pure woman and the good woman into praise for the prudish and the good-goody and the utterly unreal. Jane Sinclair, for instance, walks out on a June evening with her father and brothers and sisters, sometimes chatting with her brother William, sometimes fondling her pet white dove. She moved in a world where moth butterflies fluttered over the meadows, where 'from the low stretches of softer green arose the thickly-growing grass-stalks, having their slender ears bent with the mellow burthen of wild honey—that ambrosial feast for the lips of innocence and childhood.' When she walked out in the evening, the evening became a time when 'love would bring forth its sweetest memories and dream itself into those ecstasies of tenderness that flow from the mingled sensations of sadness and delight.' Yet to balance and excuse her unreality poor Jane Sinclair had a certain pathetic appeal, a heart broken for love, a mind crazed by love and fantastic religious scruples. Maria Brindsley the impossible heroine of *The Double Prophecy* had no such excuse. Maria's only lust was a lust for self-improvement. When her six days dressmaking ended she turned on Sunday to a day of improving reading. She 'wrote both a good hand and a good style, and was capable of keeping accounts in a clear and satisfactory manner.' When Captain Doolittle sent her the sort of letter that a Captain of that name would normally be expected to send she wrote on the envelope: 'Unopened, and rejected with indignation and scorn.' She would have been at home in some of the works of the lesser lady-novelists of that century. She certainly did not belong to the world of Denis O'Shaughnessy or Phelim O'Toole, yet there are disconcerting moments when certain characteristics of Maria Brindsley might be traced back to Cathleen Cavanagh. Cathleen had degenerated into Maria, and, when Carleton wrote that the beauty of the latter was such that he shrank from describing it, he was only confessing that he had, in several ways, lost his faculties.

But all that was very much in the future. *The Double Prophecy* was one of his lesser and later efforts and if, in that book, his praise of the good woman had ended in a eulogy for a piece of virtuous whalebone, it would be unwise to assume that the final unreality was any measure for the real good he had seen, for the real women he had known. His life was, as far as we know, surprisingly innocent. His own ideas and the conventions under which he worked tolerated no licence. But he had seen the women of Ireland in the way his mother had about her own hearth, had heard them speak forever in her voice; and always for him they walked in a world apart where the fallen merited all pity and the unstained were higher than the angels.

In that separate world he saw the love-making of the country people as they came together at fairs and markets, and all artificial backgrounds for gentle passions dried up like meadow-mist before their warm geniality. The remote, sequestered country-walk, the calm summer evening, setting suns, dewy eves, green glens and other poetical accessories had, he admitted, their value. But 'commend me to the back-room in a country public-house, of a fair day . . . to a lover, with his glass in his hand, forcing its contents into the apparently reluctant lips of his dear sweet girl, who, under a beautifully assumed feeling of offended modesty, contrives to convey to him a secret glance that is worth ten times the reckoning.'[1] In that world comic things could happen, comic words could be spoken, love could be sane as only something that is funny can be sane. Dr. McClaret could say to Emily Squander: 'I love you, dear Emily, as I do the Bible itself! I now speak of the polyglot edition. . . . For your sake I wish I were a bishop.'[2] In that world it would be 'difficult to meet a woman in whose disposition, however corrupted by evil society, and degraded by vice, there was not to be found a portion of the angelic essence still remaining.'[3] There was nothing there that Miss Edgeworth and Miss Mitford could not have found 'charming' as they found the ladies in Lever's novels 'charming,' although the malicious mind might squeeze some fun out of the possible predicament of Miss Edgeworth and Miss Mitford left alone on a desert island with Lever's Mary Draper:

> *'She'd ride a wall, she'd drive a team,*
> *Or with a fly she'd whip a stream,*
> *Or maybe sing you "Rousseau's Dream,"*
> *For nothing could escape her;*
> *I've seen her, too—upon my word—*
> *At sixty yards bring down a bird;*
> *Oh! she charmed all the Forty-third!*
> *Did lovely Mary Draper.'*

But Carleton had never known intimately the breed of Mary Draper, and the nearest approach he ever made to appreciating the masterful merits of the type was when he wrote for *The Nation* a light essay on the rights of women. Closer to him than that rampage and robustiousness was the lovely Grace Davoren[4] whose beauty like the beauty of Raftery's Mary Hynes, was, in the end, her undoing and the breaking of her heart. But he saw her lovely and innocent, dressed in her new drugget gown, her new shoes and blue stockings, striped blue-and-red petticoat displaying 'as much of her exquisite limbs' as the fashion of the day allowed. 'Her bust was perfection and her black natural ringlets fluttered about her milkwhite neck.' Then in another story,[5] describing the beauty of Nora Tyrell he stopped suddenly and laughed at himself, at the inevitable whiteness of milky necks, the inevitably-contrasting blackness of flowing and falling ringlets. He wrote: 'Her hair was

[1] *The Red-Haired Man's Wife.* [2] *The Squanders of Castle Squander.*
[3] *The Emigrants of Ahadarra.* [4] *The Evil Eye.* [5] *The Red-Haired Man's Wife.*

black as—God help me! what would an author do without the raven's wing.' For beauty could be as warm and summery as the sighs of a silly boy, sitting solitary in a hazel glen, longing for the unattainable beauty of the miller's daughter. It could be as sickly as Jane Sinclair and her pet white dove. It could be as full of sorrow as the story of ruined Grace Davoren, as full of fun as the shamble of Paddy-Go-Easy following Nancy along the road with a glance in his love-crazed eyes that was love but looked like criminal intent.

In agreement with several reputable economists he pointed out that the potato was the curse of the country. The people were dependent on the potato and the potato was particularly subject to failure and decay. There were other reasons. The potato was, when untouched by failure, easy to produce and, on that account, encouraging to early marriages. It was popularly supposed, as was the imported yellow meal, to increase fertility and to add disastrously to the population of an impoverished country. Taught by his own experience he lived to disapprove of these improvident marriages, of the light-hearted way in which the young loving couples took upon them the burdens of the world. When Peggy Donavan's father spoke with prudence against her proposed marriage with Phelim O'Toole, on the reasonable enough grounds that the O'Toole's ancestral half-acre was not enough to set up a home and family, one of the advisers on the question said with contempt: 'Are you going to make English or Scotch of them, that never marries till they're able to buy a farm and stock it, the nagers. By the staff in my hand, an Irishman ud lash a dozen o' them, wid all their prudence! Hasn't Phelim and Peggy health and hands, what most new-married couples in Ireland begins the world wid?' Phelim's father pointed out proudly that as well as health and hands and the half-acre Phelim would have also the grey goat, two stools, three hens and a toss-up for the cock, the bigger of the two pots, two good crocks, three good wooden trenchers, and HIS OWN BED. 'And my own bedstead,' Phelim added, 'an' bad cess to the stouter one in Europe.'[1]

Compared with William Carleton, Phelim O'Toole had a stake in the country, could have been as sad as the scriptural rich young man in his great possessions. Carleton tramped into Dublin as poverty-stricken as any young fellow in the whole poverty-stricken country and at the end of two years of a shiftless and uncertain existence he was married. It was a marriage made in the city, cut off by the hard crust of the pavements from the good earth and its uncountable half-acres, cut off from the market-day wooing, the

[1] 'Phelim O'Toole's Courtship' (*Traits and Stories*).

match-making, the horse-racing wedding processions, the uproarious marriage feasts of his own country. Marrying Jane Anderson in Dublin was very different from the marrying with Anne Duffy that might have been in the Clogher Valley. Defying poverty he found great happiness with Jane and with the children she brought into the world. But his heart must always have been sore remembering that he had not brought Jane gallantly home as Shane Fadh brought home his bride in the morning of the world.[1]

In the days of his bare wooing he might have wished for the aid of some match-making old woman of the breed of Biddy Brady whose art smoothed over all the obstacles between the beauty of Nancy and the pursuing, petrified stare of Paddy-Go-Easy. Biddy's high notion of her calling, leading her to maintain that the 'angel Abraham' had made the match between Adam and Eve, could have pointed out to him that 'every boy shall lave his fadher an' modher an' stick to his wife, as Adam and Eve did to one another in Parodies.' But it might have occurred to him in bitterness that being, like the old Gaelic poet, without land or wealth, cattle or horned cows, neither Biddy Brady nor Mary Murray nor any bargainer that ever spat on a palm would have undertaken his cause. For Biddy or Mary could fail in their efforts to bring bliss to the poor because a man refused to give with his son 'a slip of a pig' or a woman withheld from her daughter's dowry a pair of blankets. What, under Heaven, could any matchmaker, short of the 'angel Abraham' himself, do on behalf of a man who had neither pigs nor blankets nor half-acres, who had health but who wouldn't use his hands, who had only a jumbled half-learning and no reputation combined with pretensions to the mind of a scholar and the status of a gentleman. Back in the valley he could only have found his way to the warm heaven under the bride's pair of blankets by forcing his point through the conventional runaway match, as Alley Sheridan's lover did, a proceeding stiff with local proprieties but as effectively compromising a couple into betrothal as anything the present-day world could do in the way of untimely conceptions or discovered weekends. 'The lover,' he wrote of this custom, 'selects the house of some relation or friend of his own, and after having given notice to that friend or relation of his intention, and having gained his assent, he informs his friend of the night when he and his sweetheart will come to their house as a "running away couple"; and in order that they may not be without the means of celebrating the event with a due convivial spirit, he generally places a gallon of unchristened whiskey in their hands.'[2]

It was a simple idea and as proper as prunes and prisms, but success posited the nearness of ready friends and the availability of

<hr>

[1] 'Shane Fadh's Wedding' (*Traits and Stories*).   [2] O'Donoghue, vol. i.

home-made whiskey; and where in the homeless city could those things be found. Or where in all Dublin was there room for the great gaiety that surrounded the wedding of Shane Fadh: the Homeric race for the bottle with all the male guests whipping their horses along the road from the priest's house to claim the prize at the house of the bride's father; Billy Cormick, the tailor, arriving first even though his blood-racer jumping the last ditch, pitched him clean down the well; and the Dorans and Flanagans, in mutual vexation, battering each other with loaded whips on the street before the house; and the priest commanding them to peace in the name of the Catholic Church and the Blessed Virgin Mary and threatening to turn the two factions into stocks and stones if they persisted, with this hubbub, in delaying the dinner. Shane Fadh himself, looking back on it all like a man who remembered the gods, spoke ecstatically of the lashings of corned beef, and rounds of beef, legs of mutton, turkeys, geese, barn-door fowl, bacon, butter, potatoes, cabbage, puddings that were the favourite food, Father Corrigan carving until exhaustion and his own desire for food sent him to his chair, half a dozen gorsoons carrying cans of beer with froth on it like barm, and outside the beggars in troops on the sunny side of the ditch making short work of the leavings.

In the stony streets William Carleton remembered Shane Fadh and, maybe, spared one bitter regret for the glory that went with a wedding in the valley. His own lot was different. From Mr. Kane's classical academy he went through the streets to find his first real job—and eventually, homely lodgings—in the house of his employer, Mr. Fox, who had a lovely bass voice and a personal friendship with Henry Grattan. He had also a son who was to be Carleton's pupil and, living under the same roof, a niece, called Jane Anderson, who was to be Carleton's wife.

It is not easy to guess how many of his dreams of fair women took flesh for him in the person of Jane Anderson. According to himself Anne Duffy was nothing more or nothing less than the ideal spirit of beauty; he felt for her that love of the imagination that opens again the gates of Paradise to the exiled and expelled human race. But his love for Jane Anderson who became the mother of his children had less poetry but more reality than his love for the miller's daughter who went before him down the white road and between the green hedges, beautiful and desirable but eternally at a distance. When he created the good women of his stories, Mave Sullivan and Cathleen Cavanagh, he was happily married to Jane Anderson and the vision of Anne Duffy was as distant as boyhood or the blackbird singing in the hazel glen.

But love, as Mrs. Fox saw it in relation to her niece, needed more qualities, more foundations and leaning buttresses, than the reality that made it different from a simple poetic vision. It needed regular employment and wordly prospects, something better than chance tutoring and teaching. Mrs. Fox laughed merrily when the lodger awkwardly hinted his love, laughed with more good humour than he relished for 'the matter was above all others one on which a man would decline being laughed at.' Then Mrs. Fox tired of her own laughter, said bluntly that a man would be time enough marrying a wife when he was able to support one. So Denis O'Shaughnessy cast from him his last ambition for sesquipedalian learning, his wish to enter Trinity College; and found—through the wealthy La Touche influence—a clerkship in the Sunday School Society. He was, as might be expected, an unorthodox, independent, impatient clerk. He was also, by his own confession, an awkward, block-headed lover who 'kept hinting, and insinuating, and shaping small oracles, which no human being could understand, and that with a face that seemed better adapted for a death-bed repentance than for a lover disclosing the tender passion.' Jane Anderson, one of those great, silent women who marry odd men and manage to make them happy, saw beyond the awkwardness and unorthodoxy, into the glad heart of the boy in the strong valley, into the tortured heart of the man puzzled in the unsteady world. Opening her own heart she found room for him there, built up around him the walls of the one place in the world where he never seemed to suffer from the twisted contradictions of created things. His unorthodoxy lost him his clerkship. His aunt-in-law locked his wife in her room, locked the husband out in the street, had him removed by the watch when he attempted a forcible entry. Later when peace was restored he found himself a father, and realised dimly that around him someone had raised again the thing that went down when his father had told his last story and his mother sung her last song. 'I looked upon the world,' he said, 'as if I had been under the influence of a dream . . . but on reflecting that I now stood for the first time in a new character, that of a father, and that this was but the beginning of a fresh responsibility, which every year would call upon me to meet, I felt divided between a feeling of happiness and care: care was, perhaps, predominant, because, young as I was, I had been taught such lessons as few had ever been forced to learn.'

His learning was by no means ended. It was a poor country for a poor man with responsibilities and nothing to meet them with beyond a tattered learning that looked like a series of sesquipedalian charms.

SEVEN

'IN THOSE days,' wrote William Butler Yeats,[1] with the manner of the story-teller between the red fire and the white wall, telling of wonderful things, 'there lived in Dublin a lean controversialist, Caesar Otway. A favourite joke about him was, "Where was Otway in the shower yesterday?" "Up a gun-barrel at Rigby's."'

In those days, too, John Banim's first tragedy *Damon and Pythias* was staged by Macready in Covent Garden, and Banim, in the following year, 1822, crossed over to try his luck in London, to find after hardship and perilous experiment that the short novel was a better paying proposition than the tragedy in verse. In the same year the Reverend Caesar Otway went north from Dublin on his first visit to Donegal, to the house of a clerical friend who lived in the Barony of Kilmacrenan on land that payed rent to the upkeep of Trinity College. In the same year Charles Lever, then sixteen years of age, entered Trinity College as a pensioner, rollicked through his university courses with much high spirit but without either notable distinction or disgrace. In 1824, a qualified medical man, he was sailing for Quebec as doctor in charge of an emigrant ship, administering to the sick, gathering copy for the story of the knight of Gwynne and for the story of Con Cregan, the Irish Gil Blas, and whistling at intervals the tune about the girl I left behind me.

In 1824 the horror of the real, actual Ireland touched Tom Moore through the melodious, sentimental rose-mist that surrounded him. Anacreon, for a while, dropped his lyre to write of creeds and politics in *The Memoirs of Captain Rock*, to say that the rulers of Ireland had 'always proceeded in proselytism on the principle of a wedge with its wrong side foremost,' to compare the conciliatory advances of Irish Protestantism to Irish Catholicism to the words spoken by Lancelot to the young Jewess: 'Be of good cheer, for truly I think thou art damned.'

A year later Michael Banim was adding to the *Tales by the O'Hara Family* the blood-red story of Crohoore of the Bill-Hook; and through the land where bloody murder was as common as ditchwater Sir Walter was driving, with his head in a mist of ancient border ballads and battles, to spend—according to Thackeray's daughter[2]— 'those happy hours with Miss Edgeworth at Edgeworthstown.' The portion of Ireland that was free of poverty and reasonably detached from the more bloody purposes of the billhook welcomed Sir Walter, crowded morning after morning to his levee in St. Stephen's

---

[1] *Stories from Carleton*, with introduction by W. B. Yeats (The Camelot Series).
[2] In an introduction to *Castle Rackrent* and *The Absentee* (Macmillan, 1895).

Green, positively mobbed him when he walked down Dame Street after inspecting Dublin Castle. In August weather he drove down to Edgeworthstown and found a well-managed estate, no mud hovels, no naked peasantry, but smiling faces in a lovely land that reminded Lockhart of Goldsmith and sweet Auburn. Lockhart had momentarily forgotten that the poem about sweet Auburn was a dirge for the passing of a people. It may never have occurred to him that there was a certain connection between mud hovels and naked people and the glories of government from Dublin Castle. It did occur to him to suggest that poets and novelists looked at life chiefly as materials for their art. Sir Walter refuted him, saying: 'We shall never learn to feel and respect our real calling unless we have taught ourselves to consider everything as moonshine compared with the education of the heart.' Maria, listening with tears in her eyes, went on to compare Sir Walter to Dean Swift, much to the disadvantage of the Dean; a justified comparison for, after all, they were discussing the noble sentiments that could fall from the lips of the poor and uneducated, and the dignity of the writer's calling, and the value of such noble sentiments in the education of the heart.

Two years later, in Limerick, a young fellow who had learned in London all the hungry hack-working indignities of the writer's calling, was offering to the world three short novels under the comprehensive title *Tales of the Munster Festivals*. He wrote to a friend: 'If I can dispose of these tales to advantage, I never again, without some very urgent motive indeed, will enter London. It is grown to me . . . a place of the most dismal associations.'[1] The reviewers enthusiastically compared the tales 'in their national portraitures and sketches of manners' to the works of Sir Walter, the eminent author of *Waverley*, but the market was poor and the price low and Gerald Griffin stayed in Ireland and, in due time, burned his manuscripts and entered the Order of the Christian Brothers.

They were all peculiar, important people: the brothers Banim, the rollicking doctor called Lever, Anacreon and Captain Rock, Sir Walter with his noble sentiments and old Maria with tears in her eyes, Gerald Griffin distrusting the world more and more every day until the moment came for drastic reuniciation, the lean controversialist coming—according to the joke of the streets—out of a gun-barrel when the shower had passed, seeing suddenly a big boy from the country who had taken on his shoulders the burdens of wife and children and the attendant worries about the scarcity of money.

The thin, gun-barrel man had, in 1825, taken on himself the work of producing the first magazine ever produced in Ireland in

[1] *The Life of Gerald Griffin*, by His Brother (Duffy, Dublin, 1857).

connection with the work of the Church by law established. He called it the *Christian Examiner*, and in the work connected with it he revealed his own remarkable talents, discovered that he had himself that one wonderful talent of clear, colourful expression. For he was a scholar in antiquarian things, a gatherer of folk-lore, a man who loved travelling on lonely roads and talking with poor people, who remembered idle tales and accidental phrases, who saw lakes and mountains and the wild sea and described them so that all men could see them for ever. But, as far as Ireland was concerned, he saw the roads and lakes and mountains under a shadow, and the people as children of the shadow. It was not the shadow of landlordism living perilously on a rack-rented tenantry, nor of an established church squeezing tithes out of the tenants in spite of their poverty and against their conscience, nor of government made negative by that same landlordism and a poisonous sectarianism, nor of recurring and worsening famine and a people living precariously on one vulnerable root-crop. He saw as many of these things as it did not go against his principles to see. But any evil that he recognised as evil he attributed to the terrible influence of the Church of Rome, the scarlet woman, reaching out from her bed of luxury on the seven hills, holding in her hand the bodies and souls of the people of Ireland. His lean body was racked and feverish with hatred of the Church of Rome. The mind that treasured legends and gathered up carefully the details of antique things moved only in violent, vitriolic abuse when it turned on the Catholic priesthood, or indulgences, or the miracles of the saints. That particular form of schizophrenia has not been unusual in Europe after John Calvin. The Rev. Caesar Otway was a particularly good specimen.

The division in the man was intensified by the dozen divisions in the island on which he made his walks and wrote his sketches of travel:[1] the economic division between the small, privileged and largely irresponsible land-owning class, and the incredible mass of the tattered and destitute; the religious division between the established church of the privileged, and the persecuted Catholicism of the people; the divisions between neighbour and neighbour that had their origins in wars and conquests and plantations under Elizabeth or James I or Oliver Cromwell; the memories of ancient divisions that could still embitter and anger and destroy. Under other circumstances and in other times he might have been the complete scholarly Protestant giving invaluable service to the independent cultural life of Ireland. But in his days the Catholic mass of the people were rising up at last against the whole accumulation of penal

---

[1] *Sketches in Ireland* (1827); *Sketches in Ireland* (1839); *A Tour in Connaught* (1839); *Sketches in Erris and Tyrawley* (1841); *Eighty Years Ago in Donegal*, etc.

law and prohibition. Daniel O'Connell, with the million wiles of the perfect politician, with a voice loud enough to be heard all over Europe, came out of the mountains of Kerry; and, to the sound of men moving in thousands to O'Connell's mass-meetings all the maggots awoke in Otway's blood. In the burning atmosphere of the time with its public theological debates, its persistent contending in voice and in print over points that split Europe in the sixteenth century, Otway's name became for ever associated with men who equalled him in only one thing: an overpowering irrational hatred for that awakening of the people, a red-misted fury against the power that they saw seated in Rome. They called their movement The New Reformation; and while, from one point of view, Otway had chosen his own company, it was still his tragedy that a man loving the calm things of the mind should be swept roaring into the furnace of bigotry. With him was the Rev. Sir Harcourt Lees. (William Carleton had once rescued his setter-dog from the fury of Murphy, the strong farmer.) With him also went the Rev. Dr. Singer, the Rev. Peter Roe, the Rev. Mortimer O'Sullivan, the Rev. Samuel O'Sullivan, the Rev. Tresham Dames Gregg. The wits of Dublin laughed at them, wrote comic poems and sketches about them, for seen from the cool meadows of wit the bigot is ten times more amusing than the pedant. The Rev. Caesar Otway came in for his share of the mockery; and in return he roared as loudly as the most rabid, but always with an exquisite choice of words.

Could any one of his fellow-roarers have replied as Otway did to J.K.L. when the famous Catholic bishop[1] who wrote under those initials had accused Lord Farnham of joining in a Crusade against the people of Ireland? J.K.L.'s initial misuse of the word was not amended by anything Otway wrote, but the lean curate could be inaccurate, even idiotic, in a way that dignified inaccuracy and made idiocy suddenly sane. 'Whenever I have met the word "Crusade",' he wrote, 'there were summoned up in association with it, the images of warlike enterprise—the bearing of a bloody cross—the unfurling of the Oriflamme of extermination—the rush of infuriate multitudes breathing hatred and doing desolation—headed by some fiery priest, or Peter, or Dominic, who consecrated murder, robbery and desolation, and *said it was the will of God* . . . and if I wanted a practical illustration of my view, I might not only look down the long vista of history, to behold the sack of Jerusalem, the extermination of the Albigenses, but nearer still at the sweeping desolation of the Palatinate, or the smoking villages of the Protestants of France. But it now appears that offering to the people the lively Oracles of God—the affectionate appeal to their hearts and understandings— the expression of Christian solicitude for their soul's welfare—the

[1] John, Bishop of Kildare and Leighlin.

visit of mercy and Christian love to the house of the poor and ignorant—this is, forsooth, a Crusade.'[1]

Out in quiet country places he could now and again break away from his enthusiasm for the New Reformation, his sympathies for desolated Palatines and burnt-out Huguenots and exterminated Albigensians. He climbed a mountain in Donegal and described it so as to make it for ever Otway's magic mountain. He looked down from the mountain and saw a lake: 'Not a breath was abroad on its expanse; it smiled as it reflected the grey mountain and the azure face of heaven. . . . You could look down a hundred fathoms deep, and still no bottom: speckled trout floating at great depths seemed as if they soared in ether. . . . You might have supposed that sound had no existence here, were it not that now and then a hawk shrieked while hovering over the mountain top, or a lamb bleated beneath as it ran to its mother.'[2] Down the slope of the mountain he met Briney O'Doherty the poteen stiller and saw in him, for some reason or other, a specimen of the old Irish kern. He was a 'gaunt, grisly figure, accoutred with a bay-coloured wig, apparently made of cow's hair, and which, but half-fitting his head, moved according as he scratched it, from one side to the other, and his natural grey glibs or locks appeared; without shoes or stockings, his mouth begrimmed with the tincture of chewed tobacco.'

In the west of Ireland he saw the bog-dwellings of the Mullet where the people had brought Ireland's poverty to its logical end by living like animals in holes in the ground. The spectacle brought back to his mind a seventeenth-century jingle that showed at least that the dwelling had history behind it:

'Built without either brick or stone
Or couples to lay roof upon . . .
The floor beneath with rushes laid—'stead
Of tapestry, no bed or bedstead,
No posts, nor bolts, nor hinges in door,
No chimney, kitchen, hall or window,
But narrow dormants stopped with hay
All night, and open in the day.
On either side there was a door,
Extent from roof unto the floor,
Which they like hedgehogs stop with straw,
Or open as the wind does blow;
And though they reach from top to floor
The man crept in upon all four.'[3]

[1] A letter to J.K.L. on the subject of his Reply to Lord Farnham. By the Rev. C. Otway, A. M. (Dublin, 1827).

[2] *Eighty Years Ago in Donegal.*   [3] *Sketches in Erris and Tyrawley.*

Wherever he went he listened to stories and legends; from Mickletony O'Donnell's coloured account of how he met the fairies in the bare lands of Mayo, to the thousand legends of Saint Colmcille, tripping off the lips of every true son of Donegal. In the light of those legends he saw the ancient saint as a passionate pigeon of the church and very like a real Irishman: 'sometimes the best-humoured and softest-hearted fellow in the world, but vex him and he would kick up such a row—set all about him fighting and breaking heads like a Tipperary faction on a fairgreen.' In the light of the legends, and with the added prejudice of the minister of the established church against all forms of dissent, he saw Cromwell's soldiers as 'black mouthed troopers, greedy of gain and prodigal of blood.'

The *Quarterly Review* greeted his *Sketches in Ireland* as 'an able and delightful volume, which most certainly if Ireland were in a tranquil state, could not fail to draw thither annual shoals of tourists.' Unfortunately Ireland was not in a tranquil state, and Caesar Otway travelling the roads of Ireland saw no tranquillity among the people of Ireland whether they lived over the ground in hovels or under the ground in holes. Nor did he find any tranquillity in his own soul. For he was pursued by a ghost that was more like the ghost of Oliver Cromwell than of Colmcille, the Dove of the Cell. That ghost overtook him and overpowered him at regular intervals, and in his fever and frenzy he saw the land transformed and the very grass gone red with the power of the scarlet woman. On a ridge of high land on the border of Fermanagh and Donegal he looked down and saw a lake on either hand: the long shores of Lough Erne, where a colony of Protestant planters had made their homes; the smaller expanse of Lough Derg that had been for centuries a place of pilgrimage for Christian Europe. 'When he had looked down upon it from the mountains,' wrote W. B. Yeats, 'he felt no reverence for the grey island consecrated by the verse of Calderon and the feet of twelve centuries of pilgrims.'[1]

To say that he felt no reverence is a mild understatement. When he looked towards Lough Erne and the planted land he saw the long, lovely islands, the cultivated shores, 'the Protestant city of Enniskillen rising amidst its waters like the island queen of all the loyalty and reasonable worship that have made her sons the admiration of past and present time.'[2] But Lough Derg and its shores and surrounding mountains presented 'the very landscape of desolation, its waters expanding in their highland solitude amidst a wide waste of moors, without one green spot to refresh the eye,

[1] *Stories from Carleton*, with introduction by W. B. Yeats (The Camelot Series).
[2] *Eighty Years Ago in Donegal*.

without a house or tree—all mournful in the brown hue of its far-stretching bogs and the grey uniformity of its rocks.' On the pilgrims' island, where tradition said Saint Patrick had prayed, he saw nothing but a collection of hideous, slated houses 'which gave you an idea that they were rather erected for the recent purposes of toll-houses or police stations than anything else, and true it is they were nothing else but toll-houses which priestcraft had erected to tax its deluded votaries.' The whole thing was, as he saw it, 'the monstrous birth of a dreary and degraded superstition, the enemy of mental cultivation, and destined to keep the human understanding in the same dark unproductive state as the moorland waste that lay outstretched around.'

High in the clear air of the mountains the thin man was shaken with the horrors of unreasoning hatred. Whatever the Pope of Rome or Saint Patrick or the Catholic priesthood may or may not have done, they certainly did not create and distribute the bogs of Ireland. And when a saint wanted a quiet place in which to pray he was more likely to find it in a barren desolate country than in green occupied lands. If the tradition of centuries sent pilgrims following his footsteps that was no discredit either to pilgrims or priests. If the green land by the other long lake was now in the hands of new men, imported by conquest and the sword, that was little to the credit of the new men. If the priests were really making the pilgrimage a paying proposition, what were they doing with the money? Why did they continue to live in hideous slated houses?

Twenty additional similar considerations would have occurred to any rational man. They did not occur to Caesar Otway. He took with him from the high mountain ridge the picture of a land laid desolate by the power of superstition. That picture filled his eyes, possibly, when he wrote: 'We learn from the fountain of divine truth,that the devil is the inventor of the great anti-Christian system exhibited in the Church of Rome.' It was still in his eyes when he shook hands with William Carleton, and Carleton said that he had read the *Sketches In Ireland*, that he as a boy had made the pilgrimage to Lough Derg, that he agreed with much of what Otway had written regarding the place.

EIGHT

CAESAR OTWAY looked at William Carleton and saw the brand snatched from the burning. He listened to William Carleton's forcible talk, the stories he told of the people back in the valley, and suddenly he saw the hungry millions alive and real, living in the cabins, bending the back day after day in the small fields. Then he did two things, and one of them was good and the other evil: he suggested to William Carleton that he should write of the people as he talked of the people. For a temperament as inchoate and chaotic as Carleton's it was valuable advice. The inspiration of the precise Miss Edgeworth, that touched Sir Walter in Scotland, and Turgenev in Russia, might easily have passed over the head of William Carleton teaching in Dublin or in Mullingar in the Midlands, where he ran a school, and wrote a little for the local paper, the *Westmeath Guardian*, and had himself imprisoned for debt. Like most young writers he might readily have taken to writing of things as remote from his own experience as dukes and duchesses and captains of dragoons. Oddly and ironically enough his later works descended to that degradation, but by that time he was written out, his feet had forgotten the touch of the strong earth in the valley that had made him great. Otway's good advice meant that his first, great, enthusiastic energy set him working in the quarry out of which he himself had been cut.

Otway's bad advice talked of the service he could do to the work of the *Christian Examiner* by holding up to the light the superstitions of the people as he had seen them: the superstitions of pilgrimage and priesthood and prophecies, mass and miracles, sermons and stations and rosaries, voteens and holy wells. Carleton began suddenly to see all these things as gross superstitions, enemies of the light, enemies of the liberty of the human mind. When he sat down to write he claimed that long ago in his youth he had rejected on rational grounds all that accumulation of obscurantist things; but nowhere in his writings is there the least evidence that either in youth or maturity or age had he understood, on rational or any other grounds, the difference between one religion and another. But when he reached his right hand to Caesar Otway he could feel about his face the cold wind of poverty and hunger; he remembered the disgrace of debt, the material burdens of the man with a wife and family. Otway offered him money and the hospitality of his home, offered him also the chance to write out of his agonised bones the grudges that a man of talent can collect when he is the poor son of poor people, when he is troubled with a gipsy's prophecy and his

72

own expectation of a high destiny. William Carleton scrambled up on the fence with the firm intention of becoming a Protestant, ended up with a long leg dangling on either side of the rickety division. The one advantage was that perched on the fence with his heels kicking the air he could work and eat. Now that fence swayed to one side, now to the other, affected by the fortunes of his own people still walking confusedly on the ground. He had raised himself a little above their poverty. And some shouted at him in bitterness because he had sold them and sold his own past. And some, knowing their own heart in his heart, knowing the unsteadiness of the whole world, laughed with him when he laughed, were silent when he remembered the sorrow and the lost sunshine.[1]

Four days after Otway suggested Lough Derg as a possible subject, Carleton returned to him with the manuscript of 'The Lough Derg Pilgrim.' Otway revised it and published it. Years afterwards Carleton inserted it into the body of the *Traits and Stories of the Irish Peasantry* 'with the exception of some offensive passages.' With this story as with all those early stories it is not always possible to determine how many of the offensive passages came originally from Carleton's pen, how many were added later by Otway's editing.

In four days this novice in the writing business wrote about eighteen thousand words; four days of hard work and valuable learning and exceptionally vivid remembering.

He remembered the July morning that saw him setting out on a high intention. According to his own testimony he had a romantic mind and a morbid turn for devotion, the combination of the two leading him some time previously to try something in the way of miracles by walking out on the surface of a pond near his father's house. William Carleton failed where Saint Peter succeeded, but that watery failure naturally proves nothing, one way or the other, about miracles; proves nothing at all except that between the devotional lad who sank in the pond and the athletic lad who crossed the water by leaping Clogher Karry there is involved somewhere a subtle, significant characteristic contradiction. It is worth remembering. It was possibly part of the purposes of Caesar Otway, as was also the preliminary declaration that at nineteen years he was 'completely ignorant' of religion, although he sustained a 'conspicuous part' in the family devotions, frequently led the rosary

---

1 'From this until 1831 Carleton contributed to the *Christian Examiner*. His contributions are marked by two qualities, graphic pen-pictures and sectarian bias laid on with a trowel. The pen, fortunately, is mightier than the trowel. When Carleton is relying on his memory and upon his creative power he is interesting; when he voices opinion, he is merely shrill and monotonous. It is not difficult to visualise starvation standing at one elbow and the Reverend Caesar Otway at the other.' Roger MacHugh writing in *Studies*.

73

in the chapel, often outprayed and outfasted his bachelor uncle. There is a faint resemblance there to Denis O'Shaughnessy, and Denis for all his sesquipedalianism knew as much about religion as a stock or a stone. But Denis was wisely content when he had taken the offered kiss and the girl's heart that went with it. His creator, as ignorant at thirty as he had been at nineteen, unwisely decided to enter or was driven by necessity into, perilous polemic.

Fortunately there was something in him more powerful than polemic. There was the eye and the imagination of Denis O'Shaughnessy, the leaping devilry of philandering Phelim O'Toole, the humour that shone around Denis and Phelim and Mat Kavanagh and Ned McKeown. These things were sufficiently evident in those eighteen thousand words to make the tale they composed one of his most memorable. That morning in July, as he set off across the hills towards Petigo and the pilgrims' island, the sun shone down on him with great good humour, the upland country was around him spotted with green patches of cultivated land; the planting of mountain pine on the convex slope of a hill, the wide lake curling before the arrowy breeze of the morning, the water-fowl skimming and marking the surface of the waters, were seen and remembered for ever. His feet blistered and he removed his battered boots and went forward 'a tall, gaunt, gawkish young man, dressed in a good suit of black cloth, with shirt and cravat like snow, striding solemnly along without shoe or stocking.'

Writing in Dublin, he saw once again the first fellow-pilgrims he overtook on the road: two women with grey cloaks, striped red and blue petticoats, drugget or linsey-wolsey gowns, small white bags slung at their backs, staves in their hands. They curtsied, saw his black suit, with delicate and calculating flattery called him 'your Reverence.' The elder of the two explained her amazing agility in 'stumping along' the road in terms of prayer and the holy scapular, told him she had the heartburn all the year round except when she went to Lough Derg. When a shower overtook them as they approached a small town she threw her cloak about him, in which he 'cut an original figure, being six feet high, with a short grey cloak pinned tightly about me, my black cassimere small-clothes peeping below it—my long, yellow polar legs, unencumbered with calves, quite naked; a good hat over the cloak—but no shoes on my feet.' It was just his greenhorn's luck that his two companions were by no means the genuine pilgrims they seemed to be, that the tramping thief, who started off with such apparent auspiciousness by loaning him her cloak, ended by stealing his clothes and emptying his purse when he lay asleep in a lodging house on the return journey. But all that had really nothing to do with the pilgrimage. For a young, bumptious, self-opinionated fellow it was wonderful experience.

At Petigo the road was black with pilgrims, 'men and women of all ages, from the sprouting devotee of twelve, to the hoary, tottering pilgrim of eighty.' There was a religious tailor 'under three blessed orders'—a little man in a turned black coat and drab cassimere small-clothes, whose back was long and legs and thighs short, who walked on the edge of his feet, had a frown for eyebrows and a curve for his chin. There was a round-shouldered man with black, twinkling eyes, with plump face and rosy cheeks, a nose twisted at the top— a humorous original who smiled at everybody with infectious humour but who spoke to nobody. There was a tall, thin, important-looking personage with a severe, self-sufficient face—a classical schoolmaster who, with head pompously raised and spectacles on his nose, read in loud Latin out of the prayer-book called *The Key of Paradise*, the seven penitential psalms, to an audience of women and children and two or three men in frieze coats. There was a man teaching a woman a Latin charm against the colic, a piece of bog-latin that Carleton or Otway could easily have concocted, that could also have been the ordinary irreverent rural joke mistaken by the ignorant for a prayer: '*Petrus sedebat super lapidem marmoreum juxta eadem Jerusalem et dolebat,*' chanted the man. '*Jesus veniebat et rogabat "Petre quid doles?" Doleo vento ventre. "Surge Petre et sanus esto." Et quicumque haec verba non scripta sed memoriter tradita recitat nunquam dolebit vento ventre.*'

Chaucer would have found all these people supremely interesting, but Chaucer would never have committed the unpardonable sin of attempting to dissociate himself from his fellow-pilgrims, to scramble up to some precarious elevation and look down with contempt on them as they passed praying or singing or chatting flippantly about trivial things. Chaucer with a healthy respect for the wisdom of the crowd of ordinary men and women, could not have looked down on the grave of the martyr at Canterbury and seen only a 'celebrated scene of superstition.' But then it is never quite certain whether the man who saw Lough Derg in that way was the lanky fellow of nineteen, or the poverty-stricken fellow of thirty, or the lean minister in his late fifties who edited and revised. There is an oddly-familiar ring about the description of the road from Petigo to the lake ascending a 'hideous mountain range.' There is something more than odd in a man who had never set foot on the continent of Europe and who believed in describing only what he had seen, writing suddenly: 'Reader have you ever approached the eternal city? Have you ever from the dreary solitudes of the Campagna, seen the dome of St. Peter's for the first time—have the names of the Caesars, and the Catos, and the Scipios excited a curiosity amounting to a sensation almost too intense to be borne?' Something like this the thirty-year-old claimed for the heart of the nineteen-year-old, except that the pilgrim was 'the victim of a gloomy and superstitious dogma.' Denying his own artistic sould he abused the very colourfulness of the pilgrimage as one more snare and delusion of the Church of Rome: 'all effect, all excitement, all sensation, arising from the influence of external objects—whilst the heart is untouched, and the mind unenlightened in any sense worthy of the majesty of God, or the object of an immortal spirit.'

It might have been, it probably was, the voice of the man who lamented the Albigensians as lost and persecuted brothers. It might have been his eyes that looked ahead and saw the island with its two or three naked and unplastered slate houses, as desolate-looking almost as the desolate mountains, with its living mass of human beings appearing in the distance like worms crawling on a dead dog. It was certainly for him that the 'romance of devotion' was spoiled by the appearance of the slated houses, bringing him back to humanity, reminding him that the slated houses might have been inns, the hovels tents, and the priests jugglers. But it was Carleton himself who complained in a way that would amuse even the pilgrim of these softer times—of all that he suffered, going bare-foot around the chapel on a pavement of stone spikes, 'every one of them making its way along my nerves and muscles to my unfortunate brain.' For in that complaint there was more of Carleton's genial Old Adam than of Otway's manichaean admiration for rigid, primitive things; and the complaint recurs, twisting itself in the oddest way into the anti-papistry imposed both by Carleton's circumstances and by Otway's editing. 'For verily,' went on this story of pilgrimage, 'if mortification of the body without conversion of the life or heart—if penance and not repentance could save the soul, no wretch who performed a pilgrimage here, could, with a good grace be damned. Out of hell the place is matchless, and if there be a purgatory in the other world, it may very well be said there is a fair rehearsal of it in the county of Donegal in Ireland.'

The one unpardonable, damnable thing is that puritanical tendency to judge the hearts of other men, to see their penance as something almost obscene and masochistic, dissociated utterly from all saving repentance. The man who was to claim for himself the supreme dignity of interpreter of the people was to begin his interpretation by posing in the very false attitude of being superior to the people. The story stops for a moment to cry out: 'Oh, Romanism! Romanism! the blood of millions is upon you—you have your popes, your priests, your friars, your nuns, your monks, your hair, your teeth, your nails, your garments, your blessed buttons, your rotten bones, your bits of wood, your gold, your ivory . . . ' The list of possessions runs on and accumulates, ending up with the statement that Rome has everything except Christ. Samuel Lover and the wits of Dublin must have bent in laughter, not over the new writer, but over the familiar echo of Mr. Caesar Otway. But there is nothing in any way humorous about the pilgrim's statement that he went through the forms in the 'same mechanical dead spirit which pervaded all present.' For only incredibly ignorant presumption could in that way judge and condemn the spirits of pilgrim generations.

In the morning before the light the pilgrims went down to the water at the edge of the island, washed their hands and faces, praying while they washed. The lake water driven by the rising wind came heavily against the stony shore. There was moonlight enough to show the broken masses of black cloud passing hurriedly across the sky. The pilgrims came down in dark groups 'like shadows, stooping for a moment over the surface of the waters,' retreating again like gliding spirits. All around was the desolation of empty waters and lonely mountains, the lurid sky, the tumult of wind. Writing down that scene as he remembered it he wrote one of the most vivid of all his pen-pictures. He said that wrapped as he was in deep devotion all this had a sublime effect on his soul. He said also that the generality of those present were blind to the natural beauty, and saw it only through the medium of superstitious awe. He said that he saw a priest selling tickets for confession and, in a season of famine, refusing alms to a poor man. So William gave the man half a crown and argued with the priest who threatened him with a whip and told him he would end up a heretic.

He was William Carleton, more charitable than the clergy, more artistically and devotionally responsive to beauty than all his benighted fellow-pilgrims. We have only his word for the details of the quarrel, and his word was for ever suspect when he took alms from Caesar Otway, and, without any noticeable moral conviction, wrote abusively of everything that backgrounded the lives of the people he was to interpret.

Weighed carefully in the balance it was an unfortunate beginning for the work of interpretation. For the few years that followed, his stories were hampered and held up by a tightening tangle of contradictions. Otway's commission must have sent him raking up all the available clerical scandals. He produced the flat, tedious story of Father Butler: a young man in love with a Protestant girl, dragooned into a seminary by a scheming priest and domineering parents, and in between woeful orations about idolatry the Protestant young lady and the priested young man die in a decline. Paddy Dimnick the voteen who did his praying in the branches of a tree might have saved the story from its tedium, but for propagandist purposes poor Paddy was twisted out of all likeness to a human being. In 'The Brothers' he wrote the story of Peggy Graham who was reared a good Protestant but who departed so far from the Old and New Testaments as to make a runaway match with a Catholic. Her husband, with crude missionary intentions, made her life a hell. She had two sons: one reared a Catholic became a healthy young pagan who was breaking windows and mixing in murderous politics all the time his sanctimonious brother was advancing in grace and wisdom and Protestantism. The runaway match, that was later so gloriously and robustiously funny in the case of Alley Sheridan, was stigmatised in the case of Peggy Graham as 'an indefensible and criminal step.' The difference really was that Peggy Graham appeared in the *Christian Examiner* and Alley Sheridan in the *National Magazine*.

If no other market, no other way of making money by writing had ever been open to him, if Paddy Dimnick, and the villainous son of Peggy Graham, and Lachlin Murray who saw odd visions by a moorland lake, had really been little, unimportant people, the tangle of contradictions would have tightened. The world would never have known, never have cared. But Paddy in the tree and Lachlin on the moor had in them the beginning of greatness. They passed their message on to the valiant tailor Neal Malone who went 'blue-moulded for want of a batin''; to Denis O'Shaughnessy who walked out wonderful in the sunshine on the road to Maynooth.

NINE

'ON HIS return (from Lough Derg),' wrote William Butler Yeats, 'he gave up all idea of the priesthood, and changed his religious opinions a good deal. He began drifting slowly into Protestantism. This Lough Derg pilgrimage seems to have set him thinking on many matters—not thinking deeply perhaps. It was not an age of deep thinking. The air was full of mere debaters' notions. In course of time, however, he grew into one of the most deeply religious minds of his day—a profound mystical nature, with melancholy at its roots. And his heart, anyway, soon returned to the religion of his fathers; and in him the Established Church proselytisers found their most fierce satirist.'[1]

It is a moderately fair analysis, except for the suggestion that there were any decided dogmatic opinions to change, that he thought deliberately and over a long period. His religion was genuinely the religion of the heart. It changed with the impulses of a very impulsive heart. The link between the inner core of feeling and the outward professions could be affected even by the pressure of poverty. His creed presented no coherent, visible unity. It looked on his country and his people from a dozen different standpoints and in a dozen different ways. It revealed only the perplexity in his own soul, the chaos around him in all the land.

His cousin, John Carleton, wrote him a letter in 1841, calling him 'dear and learned cousin,' hoping that his influence would help the letter-writer to some little position that would cause him to be better known in the world, lamenting that William was so much inclined to write unfavourably of the Catholic Church. His sister Mary had written a poem of lamentation on hearing that he had forsaken the religion of his father. Reading John's letter and hearing of Mary's poem he might have remembered his father, his stainless and inoffensive life, his 'senseless and superstitious kind of piety,' his rosary-beads almost always in his hands, praying his way to the market and praying his way home again, generous and charitable in a way that went far beyond his means.[2] The senseless and superstitious part of all this was summed up in corporal mortification, which William did not approve of, and a fear of ghosts, which William might have shared. Altogether it was an admirable religion, not to be abandoned as simply and irrevocably as Mary's poem might suggest.

He could never be a turncoat after the fashion of the famous

---

[1] *Stories from Carleton*, with introduction by W. B. Yeats (The Camelot Series).
[2] O'Donoghue, vol. i.

Dr. Patrick Duigenan, the 'kiln-dried' Protestant who had publicly read his recantation of the errors of the Church of Rome, changed his name from O'Dewegenan to Duigenan, become remarkable for ever as a man of the rudest manners and the most intolerant principles. Patrick Duigenan[1] came from a poor cabin in the bleak western land of Leitrim, from the influence of a father who herded cattle and wanted his son to be a priest, from six years wandering as a poor scholar, from the patronage of a kindly Protestant clergyman, to a position at the Irish Bar and the political championship of the most rabid anti-Catholicism. A practical joker once chalked a large cross on the doctor's hat and the doctor swore vengeance on the Popish miscreant. His weird reputation gathered legends around it even to the legend that on his deathbed he had been attended by a tall, thin, austere, mysterious-looking person, of reserved appearance and foreign aspect.[2] Some said; a popish priest, a Jesuit in disguise. Some, who thought otherwise, sniffed and smelt brimstone.

Apart altogether from legend, the facts of his career show Patrick Duigenan as a typical turncoat of a time when the appalling difference between the material circumstances of Irish Catholicism and Irish Protestantism made every change to the latter from the former very naturally suspect. William Carleton was not even on the fringes of the world in which Duigenan fumed and foamed at the mouth. He was poor. His principles had nothing of the alarming steadfastness that he created for admiration in his heroine Cathleen Cavanagh. His religion was largely emotionalism. But he had a sense of fair play, a sense of honesty that led him regularly to contradict himself; and, above all, his heart remembered morning. Very accurately and easily he understood, analysed, and condemned by that analysis, the souls of such men as Patrick Duigenan, and of the many lesser men typified by Mat Purcell, the tithe proctor. 'If it weren't for the bigotry of priests and parsons,' said the proctor, 'who contrive to set the two churches together by the ears, there would be found very little difference between them . . . sorry would I be to let so slight a change as passing from one religion to another be a bar to the advancement or good fortune of any one of my children.'[3] In the eyes of Dora McMahon[4] he saw the tears of that 'ancient integrity and hereditary pride which are more precious relics in a family than the costliest jewels that ever sparkled to the sun.' Beyond a doubt he preferred always the tears of the lovely Dora to the trimming of the politic proctor. But it would be risky to assume that his admiration of one, his condemnation of the other,

---

[1] *Sketches of Irish Political Characters* London, 1799).
[2] *Irish Periodical Literature*, vol. ii, R. R. Madden (London, 1867).
[3] *The Tithe Proctor.*   [4] *The Emigrants of Ahadarra.*

fixed him unalterably in any one particular place. According to the unprejudiced opinion of Yeats his heart was always with the faith of his childhood. According to himself he knew nothing about dogmatic religion when he was a nineteen-year-old pilgrim. On all the evidence that his own writings provide he knew nothing about dogmatic religion at any period of his existence. But defying all the obvious affiliations of the heart, trying hard to ignore the bitter fact that he had first written Protestant propaganda because it paid him, he could always drop half-hints about the reality of his own conversion. The Irish Catholics did not or would not believe that any person could 'by the force of reason and judgment, see a single error in their religion, or conscientiously withdraw himself from it. Nor is this opinion confined to the lay portion of them; the priesthood in general entertain it; and, indeed, when we reflect upon the fact that they consider their church an infallible one, we do not see how they could readily hold any other.'[1]

In matters religious he was once again the boy in the valley 'perpetually leaping,' looking in at windows, craning his long neck over walls and hedges, mixing with crowds going to Mass, going on pilgrimage, finding himself suddenly in a debate that might end in violence and disturbance with the man least responsible, the man most injured. He was listening to the tramp advising Larry O'Toole, because his wife was barren and there was no heir to the half-acre, to bring her to the holy well and pray and leave behind them a token offering of a ribbon or a bit of a dress, and trust to the saint for the rest.[2] He was once again under the high cliff in the green glen, at the well of cool water below the high cascade. On the bushes around the well were fragments of cloth bleached by the weather, small wooden crosses, locks of human hair, buttons, and all the other 'fictious emblems' of property that poor people had left behind them in thanksgiving and petition. Down the glen came the blind, the lame, the pilgrim, the mendicant, the men of no children, the young people hunting fun, the paralytic carried by charitable friends. Refreshment tents were raised on the green grass, every tent with its fiddler or piper, with the symbol of its owner hoisted on the top of a pole: a salt-herring or a turf, a shillelah or an old shoe, a wisp of hay or a tattered hat. Around the well the people prayed. In the tents they ate and drank and were happy and the glen was crowded with life. 'Queen o'patriots, pray for us!' he wrote, parodying with a half-malicious affection the voices of that lost life. 'St. Abraham—go to the divil, you bosthoon; is it crushin' my sore leg you are? St. Abraham pray for us! St. Jonathan—musha, I wisht you wor in America, honest man, instid o' twistin' my arm like a gad . . .

[1] *The Tithe Proctor.* [2] 'Phelim O'Toole's Courtship' (*Traits and Stories*).

81

'My heart's curse on you! Is it the ould cripple you're thrampin' over?

'Here, Barny, blood alive, give this purty young girl a lift or she'll be undhermost.'

Or he was again on the way over the snow to midnight mass, scattered myriads of blazing torches converging on one point, a broad focus of red light that every moment extended itself more and more. It was Christmas time. Hearts were lighter and pockets heavier than at any other time of the year. Loud laughter echoed into the night from crowded shebeen-houses. On the chapel-green, Mass was said in the open air; the altar a table covered with white linen; the vested priest reading the book by torchlight; the congregation hushed and reverent, the faces touched by the strong light of the torches.

He was born a Catholic in a time when Catholics still lived under the burden of penal law. Mass was not read in the open air merely for the picturesque effect of red torches throwing their light on earnest faces, or reflecting from white snow. When he described[1] the traditional Mass of the days of penal law he was remembering what he had seen with an accurate, photographic eye, not overstraining a never very strong power for revivifying and recreating a past known only by hearsay. The wandering bishop in the story of Willy Reilly stood at an altar in a shallow cave. Outside on a grassy platform knelt the 'poor, shivering congregation.' The weather was stormy, with hard frost and snow. 'The position of the table-altar saved the bishop and the chalice and the other matters necessary for the performance of worship, from the direct fury of the blast . . . but occasionally a whirlwind would come up, and toss over the leaves of the missal in such a way, and with such violence, that the bishop, who was now trembling from the cold, was obliged to lose some time in finding out the proper passages. It was a solemn sight to see two or three hundred persons kneeling, and bent in prostrate and heartfelt adoration, in the pious worship of that God that sends and withholds the storm; bareheaded, too, under the piercing drift of the thick-falling granular snow, and thinking of nothing but their own sins, and that gladsome opportunity of approaching the forbidden altar of God, now doubly dear to them that it *was* forbidden.'

The sufferings, the heroic endurance of that dark time bound him with bonds of strong sympathy to the faith of the people. But actually within his own memory there were sunny Sunday mornings spent with the boys in the valley, waiting the arrival of the priest, as the people waited outside the square, unornamented, slated house that was the chapel of Knockimdowney.[2] In little groups

---

[1] In *Willy Reilly*.   [2] 'The Battle of The Factions' (*Traits and Stories*).

the congregation lay on the chapel-green, telling stories, talking politics, criticising the neighbours; or gathered in a circle around the loquaciousness of the local schoolmaster; or, to the chagrin of the schoolmaster, around a wandering story-teller or a sanctimonious vagrant 'repeating some piece of unfathomable or labyrinthine devotion, or perhaps warbling, from stentorian lungs, some *melodia sacra* in an untranslateable tongue.' Nosegays of girls sat on the green, sunny banks, or sat like bachelor's buttons in smiling rows criticising the young men as they passed. Those who walked barefoot to the chapel would retire modestly behind a hedge to prepare for exhibiting to the best advantage their bleached thread stockings, well-greased slippers, well-turned ankles and neat legs which 'my fair countrywomen can show against any other nation living or dead.'

Or he could hear echoing in his ears the voice of Kelly in the station-house racing along at the Latin of the *Confiteor* under the examination of the priest: 'Confectur Dimniportenti batchy Mary semplar virginy, batchy Mackletoe Archy Angelo batchy Johnny Bartisty, sanctris postlis . . . '

'"Very well, Kelly," said the priest, "right enough, all except the pronouncing, which wouldn't pass muster in Maynooth, however. How many kinds of commandments are there?"

'"Two, sir."

'"What are they?"

'"God's and the Church's."

'"Repeat God's share of them."'

From those pictures, from the scores of pictures that could be taken at random from his stories, no man would be foolhardy enough to define in a paragraph the exact attitude of Carleton to the Catholicism to which his heart always belonged. It was the faith of the people and he was the interpreter of the people. It was the faith of the poor and persecuted, and his heart felt for the poor and was proud of that past in which persecution had been successfully resisted. It was the faith of his childhood and no man ever gloried so much in making the journey of the heart backwards into the world he had known as a child. It was the faith of the priests; and priests, good and not so good, crowd in dozens across the pages of his books. His own disposition led him to criticise, as naturally as Chaucer criticised, the Church to which he naturally belonged. But Chaucer's time was a settled time, of solid, established values. There was no spirit of disorder to send the Canterbury pilgrims wandering for ever in an uneasy world, never reaching the tomb of the martyr, never properly understanding the motive of their journey, the mystical meaning of all pilgrimage.

Evory Easel, the good landowner disguised as the questioning English visitor, said in *Valentine McClutchy* to Mr. Clement, the Protestant minister: 'Is there not an extensive system of conversion proceeding, called the New Reformation? It appears to me by the papers, that the Roman Catholic population are embracing Protestantism by hundreds.' The answer to his question was that the great spiritual principle sustaining the reformation movement was the failure of the potato crop. The knavery or distress of two or three Catholics 'who were relieved, when in a state of famine, by a benevolent and kind-hearted nobleman, who certainly would encourage neither dishonesty nor imposture' set the reformation going. And out of conversion through hunger, and as a sort of sideshow for the agitation for Catholic emancipation, came the public theological debates carried on at great length and with heat all over the country. Mr. Clement looked upon these debates as manifestations of fanaticism and bigotry, and productive only of lamentable evil, inflaming the worst passions of opposing creeds, disturbing social harmony, poisoning moral feelings. As far as Mr. Clement—or William Carleton—knew there was no instance on record of either side having made a genuine convert by this method of public debate.

More than a century afterwards, in clearer air and more plentiful times, the truth about the conversions of the belly and the uselessness of loud, bitter, public debate is obvious enough. It was not so obvious when seen dimly through the red haze of hunger, when heard faintly over the noise of agitation and argument that entangled religion with politics and politics with religion leaving a woeful tradition from which modern Ireland has not completely escaped.

When Darby O'Drive,[1] the rascally bailiff, circulated for the devilment of the thing, the report that the New Reformation Society was ready to receive converts at the rate of five guineas a head, there was a threefold response in the neighbourhood of Castle Cumber. First and fastest along the road that led to the minister's house went the profligate and unprincipled, spurred on to speed by cold, nakedness and famine, hindered by no burden of moral and religious principle. Following them went 'the simple and honest poor who had no other way of avoiding all the rigours and privations of that terrible season, than a painful compliance with the only principle which could rescue themselves and their children.' Dancing in the rear went the wags, with empty bellies and ragged backs, enjoying the whole ludicrous business of reading recantations, renouncing Popery as a capital spree 'and a thing that ought to be encouraged until better times came.'

Like some fantastic death-dance in a medieval dream they came

---

[1] *Valentine McClutchy.*

to the house of Mr. Phineas Lucre who thought more of the golden guineas than of all the possible or probable converts between Castle Cumber and the Crimea. Nick Feasthalagh offered himself and his family of six for immediate re-christening into Protestantism as an alternative to death by starvation. He explained that he had been *in* on suspicion of the burning of Nugent's hay, but, by the five crosses, he was innocent, for the court couldn't prove it and he came out with flying colours, glory be to God. He pointed out that he would make a good Protestant when he came to understand it, that he would be 'dam useful in fairs or markets to help the Orangemen to lick ourselves, your honour, in a skrimmage or party fight, or anything of that kidney.' Barney Grattan, entering with his wife Rosha, said he had been thinking a great deal 'about these docthrines and jinnyologies that people is now all runnin' upon,' for he could tell a story at a wake as good as any man in the five parishes. Rosha, less discreet, confessed that they had been converted by the accounts that were abroad of young preaching gentlemen from Dublin who were so full of learning and so rich. Following the crowds, drawn by the attraction that crowds have for the fool, came the gigantic Raymond of the Hats, to terrify Mr. Lucre by suddenly seizing the Bible, putting it to his nose, smelling it and shuddering and crying out: 'It's dripping with blood—here's murder on this page—there's starvation on that.' Turning the pages, he commented with the terrible wisdom of the unbalanced mind, telling of madness and sick children, of poor people turned out of their homes to the shelterless roads, of cattle and stock seized and impounded and children crying with hunger, of farms left empty and lonely because the landlord's agent had evicted the rightful tenants and no other men had the courage to move into their places, of wickedness between neighbours, and murder, and young foolish lives lost on the scaffold. Throwing from him the misused word of God the fool cried out that it should not make him as wicked as other men, then asked Mr. Lucre for the loan of his religion until the new praties came in.

Out on the open road Darby O'Drive, convert to Protestantism, had come through wild words to wilder blows with Bob Beatty, convert to Catholicism. For Darby aspired to the keepership of the local gaol, and Father McCabe was reputed to have cured Bob's epilepsy. The people came running from the fields. The battle developed and spread. Although the course of the argument that preceded the fight had led the two men to support each the religion to which he had originally belonged, the Catholics fought for Bob and Protestantism, the Protestants 'owing to a similar mistake fought like devils for Darby and the Pope.'

In quiet moments he could admire the orderliness of the Presbyterian Sabbath as he saw it among his friends in the north-eastern portion of the country. But when Randy O'Rollick[1] commended that Sabbatarianism because it bestowed 'no privilege of licentiousness and crime,' allowed no profane songs after dinner, no gambling, no card-playing, no riotous entertainments, he was very far away from the character so obviously intended for him when he was given a name. He was even farther away from the true character of his creator who could forget altogether the work of a writer in the passion of the time for being morally instructive. He was also quite falsely implying that other non-Presbyterian churches did grant that Sunday privilege of licentiousness and crime. Randy, again in that meditative, unrandyish, unrollicking mood, found a remarkable difference between 'the feeling observable in a Protestant or Presbyterian place of worship and that which prevails in a Roman Catholic chapel.' Assuming that Randy O'Rollick would have noticed the difference between grades or varieties of devotion his analysis of that difference was unlikely to go far unchallenged in any part of Ireland. It could not even go unchallenged very far through the written works of William Carleton. Randy found in the Presbyterian meeting-house 'a higher and more enlightened perception of religious influence, associated more with reason than with feeling,' in the Catholic chapel 'more impulsive piety.' The religion of the Protestant, as he saw it, was more of the head; that of the Roman Catholic more of the heart. 'In the one there exists a reasoning principle which operates beneficially upon all the faculties, as well as upon the business of social life—in the other the feeling is stimulated by forms and ceremonies which are not understood; but the moment religion is approached as a matter of investigation, the influence of reason is suspended, an interdict is laid on it so far as the dogmas of the church are concerned, and the right of private judgment being denied upon that subject, it is not likely that the individual will be trained to habits of independent thought upon any other.'

He died in 1869 outside the Church into which he was born. The judgment of Randy O'Rollick was written down in 1851. If it is to be taken as Carleton's final decision, then he died also outside the Church to which, according to his own opinion, he quite obviously belonged. For no man ever used his reason less in matters of faith. He used every impulse of the heart including the natural desire of a father to protect his family from the material hardship of a very meagre world. But he was a million miles of the mind away from the cold wisdom of Aquinas proclaiming that reason had in man the dominating place. He was the perplexed pilgrim losing his

[1] *The Squanders of Castle Squander.*

balance at the beginning of the journey, staggering on in dizzy bewilderment, anxious to please and to pacify as he went, anxious to tell the truth but not always finding it possible, offending all men by the erratic uncertainty of his progress. He wanted to stand high above all the confusion, in some cool rational place. But the fact that he had once walked in the procession to the house of Mr. Phineas Lucre, taken his guineas or the proverbial soup with the unfortunate minority of his fellow-countrymen convinced by the crushing power of material things, always retarded his ascent. All around him was the confusion of the fight between Darby the Bailiff and Bob, the cured and converted epileptic, the uncanny confusion of the mind of the fool. All along the road on which pilgrim and procession passed the walls and houses were falling down, the hedges withering, the fields black with decay.

TEN

TOWARDS THE end of January, 1801, the United Parliament of Great Britain and Ireland assembled in London. In the new House of Lords the peer who had once threatened to tame his fellow-countrymen into the likeness of cats treated his new audience to a violent attack on those fellow-countrymen, gave his blessing, such as it was, to the outrages that had provoked and crushed the rebellion, advocated for Ireland enlightened government through perpetual martial law. It was an exquisitely appropriate commencement for the Irish nineteenth century. It was a poor way for Ireland to introduce herself into London's parliamentary debates; and Pitt, whispering to Wilberforce, asked him in the name of God had he ever listened to such a rascal.

In the following year the rascal, whose name was Lord Clare, died in Dublin of perfectly natural causes, and around his house in Ely Place the people made jubilant and insulting din, and on his coffin at the graveside the remembering crowd flung dead cats. Outside a church in narrow Thomas Street the body of Robert Emmet was set swinging on a scaffold, and the people of Ireland had found the most romantically coloured of all Ireland's hanged heroes: the young man who had loved Ireland to the point of sacrificing his life in a rebellion that degenerated into an undignified street scuffle, who had loved a woman to the point of again risking, and this time losing, his life in an effort to see once again her beloved face; who had cried out that no man was to write his epitaph until Ireland was a nation.

For good or evil the phrase was to remain in the troubled Irish memory. Young men used it as young men will always use a phrase that came so nobly from the lips of a man who died heroically and was also young. Prudent men judged it as prudent men will always judge the words of those who foolishly and with reckless hope sacrifice all things, sacrificing even life. Cynical men laughed over it as cynical men will always laugh over the wild ideal, the rhetorical definition of the unattainable. A dozen varieties of nation-makers and nation-breakers stood in their dozen different relationships to that phrase, the man who made it, and to all that he represented. Principally, within the active lifetime of William Carleton there were Daniel O'Connell, and Thomas Osborne Davis and the young men of the Young Ireland movement.

Judged by the romantic standards of Young Ireland, O'Connell, the great agitator, had in his worst moments all the low, native cunning of the peasant. The suggestion was unjust to O'Connell and unjust to the peasant. In a distant Kerry valley, on the edge of an ocean that opened across to a continent where Catholics could be educated and from which wines could be smuggled, O'Connell learned his first lessons in an uncanny understanding of the Irish people. But he learned those lessons not as one of the poor in poor cabins knowing neither the taste of wine nor the advantages of a continental education. He had all the chances that the irregular and never quite legal life of the Catholic gentry could give him. He was so close to the continent that he almost inevitably became a continental figure in a way impossible to Davis or John Mitchel or Charles Gavan Duffy. He had cunning, but it was the cunning of the trained lawyer knowing every trick and able to avail himself of every chance, able to force the united Parliament to grant to Catholics those rights that the Parliament had never particularly wanted to grant, able to stand up over and dominate his own people, as big in their eyes as a mountain in his native Kerry, until in the end the incredible extent of that domination brought down O'Connell and with him the whole generation that he had ruled like a king.

Only one other man alive at that time understood as intimately as O'Connell did the hearts and souls of the Irish peasantry. He did not dominate them from a platform, using his knowledge to build up his own might or to gain relief for the oppressed or to lay, almost incidentally, the foundation on which so much of modern Ireland is built. But he wrote his knowledge of them into memorable stories, gathering to himself for all time the hearts of those who love good stories about their own people. He described them as he saw them, sometimes forgetting his high calling as story-teller in various contradictory efforts to be with the builders of a new nation and the planners of a new time. He could not fail to see them gathered around platforms in green places, specially chosen for historically sentimental appeal, enslaved by the voice of the great tribune who came like thunder out of the mountains of Kerry. He deplored in words of unmistakable bitterness both the thunder and the enslavement. Possibly he was enviously angry at seeing another man holding such power over his people. More likely he was feeling, not the bitterness of an unsuccessful claimant to a throne already filled, but the frail anger of the weak against the man who ruled and the man who led. He was resenting O'Connell, as the people of Ireland have always resented their leaders even when following them into foolishness and confusion and death.

'Agitation,' wrote Carleton, looking up from somewhere in the crowd at the enormous gesturing figure of one of the greatest of all agitators, 'may be sincere without being honest; sincere in its purpose but dishonest and unscrupulous in its means.' In the noble, unsuccessful Henry Grattan he could see none of O'Connell's trickery, his leer and grimace and dexterous manipulation, 'no tongue in the cheek, no plastic and dishonest adaptation to circumstances nor any shameful departure from expressed opinion, or avowed principle.' The condemnation of the Great Dan for lack of consistency came rather oddly from a man that most of Dan's followers would have described quite simply as a turncoat. But it reflected at least his own high idea of his own high principle. It showed that on occasion he could judge political things with all the shrewd cunning of the Irish peasant that he really was. O'Connell understood that cunning as he understood everything else in the Irish people; he used it for his purposes, but he did not possess it. For he failed foolishly in the end with all the ludicrous, grandiloquent foolishness of the gentleman born in the big house, educated on the continent, reared on the flavour of smuggled wine; and, dying on the continent, he willed his heart to Rome, his decaying body to his decaying, desolate country.

Over the terrifying spectacle of that failure Carleton from the cabins wrote: 'I admit Mr. O'Connell's vast talents, his superhuman perseverance, and his incredible labours. But he fell a victim to his own power and was gradually corrupted by the slavish credulity of the people, who became blinded to his political errors, and looked upon his changes of principle only as necessary manoeuvres against the enemy. Had that man by the power of any great revolution, become a monarch, he would have become a tyrant. As it was, he could bear no man but a slave about him . . . '

With all his inability to look steadily at creeds and politics, accepting and rejecting on some solid, consistent rational basis, William Carleton was no slave. It was the largest part of the poetic message of the men of Young Ireland that no man, particularly no Irishman, should be a slave. And when William Carleton rebelled against Caesar Otway as he had rebelled against the authority of the Catholic priest he was influenced to a certain extent by the one characteristic which he had in common with Young Ireland. Possibly he was more powerfully influenced by the demand of his own genius for freedom from an editor who was so zealously lacking in taste as to be capable of turning creations like Denis O'Shaughnessy and Phelim O'Toole into preachers for the New Reformation. It was only to be expected that Denis would depart from Caesar Otway as he had departed from Maynooth, that Phelim would rise up and fly from the New Reformation as he fled from the several deluded women to whom he had vowed love and devotion, that their creator would desert the lean controversialist for better reasons but with as little ratiocination as he displayed when he left the Catholc Church.

On the fifteenth day of October, 1842, the first number of the

Nation newspaper appeared, the three men mostly responsible for its appearance being Davis from Munster, Dillon from Connaught, Duffy from Carleton's own province of Ulster. His friendship with Duffy, who had left Monaghan as Carleton had left Tyrone to go on the world and seek his fortune, brought him easily into contact with the complete circle of romantic revolutionaries. He respected their high principles, and despised most of their methods and a large proportion of their ideas. Duffy, who was a long way from being a helpless romanticist, who held to his high principles and in spite of adversity used the world to his own advantage, was convinced that Carleton 'with all his splendid equipment of brains was incapable of comprehending' those revolutionary ideas. But whether he despised them through prudence or native cunning or intellectual inability to know what they were about, he was influenced by those men in a remarkable way, in a way that added value and violent strength to his own work, showed him for ever in a different light to the eyes of his own people.

In its seventh number the *Nation* contradicted, at Carleton's request, an 'absurd rumour' that Carleton alone and unaided was writing the whole newspaper. The request was as absurd as the rumour; but it displays his offence-avoiding anxiety to dissociate himself from the political principles of a paper to which he actually afterwards contributed; and, the way in which the request was dealt with, displays the high place that Carleton's stories had already gained for him in the estimation of the men who wanted, according to the formula, to make Ireland a nation. They said that if Carleton had actually written the whole paper they would have been proud of that fact to the point of boasting. 'There is not in the empire,' they said, 'a periodical which would not be honoured by having the name of Carleton amongst its contributors. It will be said that he has wronged and misrepresented the people of Ireland, their religion and their clergy; we acknowledge the fact, and we lament it—not more deeply, however, than does Mr. Carleton himself.'

That was almost a public recantation of Caesar Otway and all his works and pomps. It was certainly a public appeal to the people from the man who, with the *Traits and Stories* and *Fardorougha The Miser* already to his credit, was justifiably beginning to regard himself as the interpreter of the people. He was anxious that they should see him as he saw himself. So he sat down and wrote the stormy story of Valentine McClutchy and Solomon McSlime, catching in its terrible pages the differences and dissension that split Irish life in twenty different directions, dividing the people so completely that, even a century after the time in which he presented the story for serialisation to the owners of the *Nation*, Emmet's epitaph remains unwritten.

91

Thomas Davis objected to the serialisation idea, seeing the force of the story being more effective if published as a book. In 1845 it was published as a book. In 1846 a French translation appeared in Louis Veuillot's paper *L'Univers*. What it meant was that Carleton, who so perfectly understood the manners and customs of the people, had really come to close grips with the problems that perplexed their lives. From several points of view it is the most important book of the Irish nineteenth century.

The people existed precariously on the land, an almost completely agrarian community. They were at the mercy of the owners of the land who in most cases cared nothing about the people, nothing about the country in which they lived, except in so far as their rack-rented tenants provided them with money to spend in London or in pleasure places on the continent. The people were mostly Catholic in religion but the tithe-demands of a Protestant state-established Church pushed them down still deeper into the dirty swamp of poverty and misery and ignorance. Their hunger left them little protection against rabid proselytisers ready to buy a very literal lipservice to Protestantism with offers of hot soup and good potatoes. They were at the mercy of the armed forces of the bitter and bigoted thing that called itself Orangeism, and Orangeism, except in periods of special enlightenment, had the approval and encouragement of men in high places. The poor man on the land could go out from this through the door beginning to open into American places, or he could seek relief through reprisals: murder or robbery or destruction of property. The remedy was worse than the disease. It meant that the government of Ireland was one act of repression and coercion after another, and those who suffered from repression and coercion were logically enough those who had had no official approval in the committing of outrage.

That was the social and political and economic background to the lives of Carleton's people. It was the gallows under which they danced with the wild irresponsibility of men daring death and the devil to do their worst. It was the great cloud that overhung their merriment and their sorrow, their singing and love-making, and going on pilgrimage. The religious hates of the sixteenth century, the imperialism that came to life in the eighteenth, the cant of law and landed property and economic necessity that draped like a heavy cloak over the sins of the nineteenth, came together and festered on one small island on the fringe of Europe. Witnessing the unholy meeting, waiting and watching for every favourable moment were the black shadow of hunger, the red shadows of murder and sudden death.

The English visitor who came to Ireland with a really observant eye and a belief in the necessity of justice could find out extraordinarily illuminating things. Phil McClutchy, the worthy son of Val the Vulture, drawing three yellow fingers across his chin in a secret sign of Orangeism, pointed out to Evory Easel, the visitor, that being a member of the Church of England or the Church of Ireland was scarcely sufficient unto salvation. 'The great principle here,' he said, 'is to hate and keep down the Papists, and you can't do that properly unless you're an Orangeman. Hate and keep down the Papists, that's the true religion.'[1] Evory Easel, with the great gift of an enquiring mind, investigated both the theory and the practice of the Orangeism of Castle Cumber and Val McClutchy, which was also the Orangeism of the nineteenth century and, with the addition of a great deal of respectability, the Orangeism of the present day. In the qualifications laid down by rule as essential for the good Orangeman he saw that it would be 'almost impossible, to find in any organised society, whether open or secret, a more admirable code of qualifications.' But these excellent abstract moral and religious principles had absolutely no influence on the practical working of the society. Its sole purpose seemed to be to 'inflame the passions of the lower classes of Protestants,' stimulating them 'too frequently, to violence, and outrage, and persecution itself, under a conviction that they are only discharging their duties by a faithful adherence to obligations.'

It was more natural for the novelist, more entertaining for his readers than the English visitor's dry comment on Orange rules and Orange practice, to follow McClutchy's yeomanry when they plundered houses in an alleged search for arms or met together in blunt and plain-spoken council. Solomon McSlime in all his glory attended the Castle Cumber lodge-meetings less as an active participant than as a pious and edifying influence, drinking whisky punch with them to counteract any tendency to pride, rewarded after the humility of the third cup by 'an easy uprising of the spiritual man,' by a greater sense of inward freedom, and an elevation of soul.[2] Solomon McSlime was the conventional hypocrite or a caricature of the conventional hypocrite, praying prayers over the poor that he robbed, psalm-singing over the servant-maids he seduced. But the conventional hypocrite and the Irish Orangeman had, and have, a common possession in a naïveté about which it is very easy to be obviously funny. Bob Clendinning,[3] the typical ordinary Orangeman, reacted violently against the suggestion that his rule of life would ever allow him to cheat a Papist. 'No,' Bob bellowed from the bottom of his honest Orange soul, 'I'd chate no man; no, no—a'm not that bad aither. A'd fight a Papish, a'd

1 *Valentine McClutchy*.   2 *Ibid.*
3 *The Squanders of Castle Squander*.

lick a Papish, an' a hope a'll help to drive them out of the country yet. No sir; my name's Bob Clendinning, but a'd chate no man. A know my duty better.'

When McClutchy's yeomanry had completed the ransacking of the house of a Catholic who had the misfortune to be a personal enemy of the great Valentine, one armed man asked for something to drink as a reward for the unusual civility with which they had treated their victim. They hadn't broken his doors and furniture, or stabbed bayonets into his beds or bed-clothes. But another raider roared that he'd drink no Papish whisky, because it was—as every well-instructed Orangeman knew—specially blessed and christened at the hands of the priest. The grounds on which one man claimed the whisky and those on which another rejected it may seem fantastic even in a fantastically unsettled period. But William Carleton remembered the night his sister had cried in pain, stabbed in bed by an Orange bayonet; and, in twentieth-century Belfast, a high Orange official prohibited under severe penalties the members of Orange lodges from slaking their thirst in public houses owned by Catholics.

ELEVEN

IN 1830 Maria Edgeworth had written a letter to her brother complaining that she no longer found it possible to write about Ireland. 'Realities' were 'too strong, party-passions too violent to bear to see or care to look at their faces in a looking glass.' In that same year Charles Lever undertook the editorship of the *National Magazine and Dublin Literary Gazette*; and Brooke, the Dublin publisher, put on the market in two octavo volumes the first series of the *Traits and Stories of the Irish Peasantry*. These two volumes contained the pleasant humour built up around Ned McKeown and his wife Nancy, the echo of the Gaelic story-teller in the adventures of Jack Magennis of the Routing Burn, the homeric episodes of Shane Fadh's wedding and Larry McFarland's wake. They echoed with all the fun of Mat Kavanagh and his tattered scholars sitting in a circle in the subterranean schoolhouse of Findramore; stiffened with horror in the stories of the horse-stealers, of the murder that happened after midnight mass and the dead body that spoke against its murderer, of the woman possessed by a demon lover. They followed the tide of the terrible battles of factions and parties. They followed the adventures over the sea in England of Phil Purcell the Pig-Driver and his drove of pigs, as lean and wild and hungry as wolves, coming like an Egyptian plague on the fat English farmers who were unfortunate enough to buy them.

It was an Ireland of which Maria Edgeworth really knew very little. But she knew enough to recognise in time the genuineness of Carleton's testimony. Her confession of inability to write any longer about Ireland had nothing at all to do with the ivory tower, for living not in an ivory tower but in a big house, understanding thoroughly the dominant minority that ruled Ireland from the big houses, her native powers of perception led her to feel uneasy about the future of a country so bitterly divided against itself. The earth was shaking with the first shock of an earthquake that would bring the big houses flat to the ground, for the men and women who lived in those houses did not see that the security of their own lives could only continue by finding new foundations in justice, in the security and prosperity of a free people.

The man who published in the year of Miss Edgeworth's despair the stories of Mat Kavanagh and Larry McFarland and Shane Fadh, went on some years later to give concisely the reason for the passion and bitter unease that had disturbed the authoress of *Castle Rackrent*. 'The laws of agrarian property,' he wrote, 'are the laws of a class; and it is not too much to say, that if the rights of

95

this class to legislate for their own interests were severely investigated, it might appear, upon just and rational principles, that the landlord is nothing more nor less than a pensioner upon popular credulity, and lives upon a fundamental error in society, created by the class to which he belongs.'[1]

In a normally-balanced society there would be nothing revolutionary about the ideas expressed in those words. But even more obvious truths had touched sensitive spots and aroused resentments among the peculiar people who owned the land of Ireland. The magistrates of County Tipperary had grown red in the face with anger at the villainy of Thomas Drummond, an honest man from Scotland made, by the laughter of God and the coming to power of Lord Melbourne's Whig administration, Under-Secretary at Dublin Castle, when he told them that property had its duties as well as its rights. Neither Thomas Drummond nor William Carleton had advanced to the place where they could realise that long neglect of duties must cancel all claim to rights. Thomas Drummond was an honest man, but he was a government official paid to build up and preserve, not free to make his way to the new world through the destruction of the old. Thirty years after his time it was obvious enough that the old world had very diligently managed to destroy itself. William Carleton was a novelist, neither by nature nor inclination a revolutionary thinker. His plan for a better Ireland would have preserved landlords educated to the consciousness of their own responsibilities and duties; tenants educated to their own proper value in society, instructed in their moral and civil duties, no longer labouring under that 'humiliating and slavish error, that the landlord is everything and themselves nothing.'[2]

About the same time a man called James Fintan Lalor was saying quite simply that the land belonged to the people in spite of landlordism and Castle government, because God who made the earth had granted it to Adam and his poor children for ever and ever. It was a simple, utopian teaching. It was laughably, pitiably out of place against a background of a nation of tattered cottiers, poverty-stricken, living under the threatening and thickening shadow of hunger. But, after several decades of further suffering and famine and emigration and incredibly cruel evictions, a one-armed man called Michael Davitt came to educate the remnant of William Carleton's Irish people to a sense of their own proper value in society. Davitt in the course of one lifetime had lived in three separate hells: in the world of cabins where a landlord's caprice could fling a family, young and old, well and ill, out in any weather on the homeless roads; in the whizzing, roaring world of developing English industrialism where an accident could leave a man maimed for life;

[1] *Valentine McClutchy.*   [2] *Ibid.*

in the prisons in England where a man could find himself for recklessly telling the truth about Ireland. But great suffering only taught him greater sympathy for those who suffered, taught him, also, the gospel of manhood that he passed on to the people, that William Carleton saw partially and incompletely as something desirable, that Miss Edgeworth may have heard, with the intuition of a woman who was also a genius, rudely threatening the existence of the only world she knew.

The day of manhood and rude resistance was not yet. William Carleton saw his own people, among themselves as splendid as Shane Fadh or as honest as Owen McCarthy or as comic as Phelim O'Toole, walk hatless before the squire's agent, or cringing and slavishly humble in the shadow of the big house. They gave their duty-labour and their glove-money to exacting, rapacious masters. A poor man's corn could be drop ripe, his hay at the precarious state that cried out for saving, his turf undrawn and lying in the bog; and, while he bent his back doing unrewarded duty-labour for the landlord or the agent, his own corn and hay and turf might be lost. Afterwards he had his rent to pay. He had also to collect enough glove-money to bribe the agent at regular intervals to renew his lease, the giving of glove-money being no guarantee that the renewal for which the bribe had been taken would actually be granted.[1] Even when menaced neither by immediate poverty or hunger every detail of the poor man's life and of the life of his family rocked and reeled with a terrible insecurity. There were the recurrent fears and humiliations of gale-day at the house of the landlord or his agent. On such occasions the tenant displayed nothing 'of that erect freedom of demeanour and natural exhibition of goodwill, which characterise conscious independence, and a sense of protection.' On the part of the agent or landlord there was only 'a contemptuous hardness of manner, a vile indifference, and utter disregard of the feelings of those by whom he is surrounded, that might enable the shallowest observer to say at a glance, here is no sympathy between that man and those people.'[2]

It was symptomatic of the whole disordered society that so much that was terrible and pitiable and devilish accumulated around the day of ignominy on which the people who lived with difficulty on the land paid their rent to those other people who lived by the land. Describing gale-day in McClutchy's office at Castle Cumber, Carleton saw a whole section of Ireland pass before his eyes like a dance of death. There was the poor tenant whose only crime was his poverty, bowing his head in shame before the insolent invective of

1 'The Poor Scholar' (*Traits and Stories*).
2 *Valentine McClutchy*.

97

the agent: a generic study of the oppressor and the oppressed. There was a man with murder in his eyes listening to the words that told him that henceforward he would have no home, no shelter even for himself or his wife or children. There were the more comfortable farmers 'who were able to meet their engagements, but who laboured under the galling conviction that, however hard and severely industry might put forth its exertions, there was no ultimate expectation of independence—no cheering reflection, that they resided under a landlord who would feel gratified and proud at their progressive prosperity.' There were farmers who could meet their engagements only by the sacrifice of all domestic comfort, who slept on bad beds, ate little food, wore tattered clothes, who practised falsehood and hypocrisy through the stern necessity of concealing even a good coat from the agent's eye in case their rents would be raised to punish the effrontery of 'getting fat, impudent, and well dressed on his Lordship's property.'

Deeper down in distress were the tenants who, in their desperate effort to pay the rent and keep a roof over their heads, sold their meal and wheat and oats at ruinously low prices, who came to their day of reckoning 'ill clad, ill fed, timid, broken down, heartless.' Deeper still were those who came in shivering raggedness to plead for mercy, with downcast eyes that spoke of keen and cutting misery, eyes that were dead and hopeless in expression: the grandfather accompanied by his grandsons, the widow whose difficulties might be increased if she were 'handsome herself, or the mother of daughters old enough, and sufficiently attractive, for the purposes of debauchery.' Randy O'Rollick, who so often spoke and acted in a way that belied his name, discovered while Squire Squander's family was absent in London the difficulties of four women who had borne bastards to the squire's two sons; and Randy meditated on the grievous conditions that could tempt 'otherwise virtuous' girls to sell themselves for the promises of the landlord's son that the next gale of rent would be remitted or reduced.[1] He saw, with a vision that would further have disturbed Maria Edgeworth, the curse and judgment of God coming on the landlords and their families.

In Esthonia, when, with a pedantry possibly inherited from her father, she was annotating *Castle Rackrent*, Maria discovered that the Sclavonian race of peasant slaves paid tribute to their lords on lines similar to the Irish duty-work and duty-fowl. But although the Sclavonians, possibly remembering a day when feudalism did actually imply reciprocal obligations, ingenuously called this tribute by a word that meant 'righteousness,' they did not seem particularly happy about the whole business. For an old Esthonian rhyme

[1] *The Squanders of Castle Squander.*

abused the gentry as the cause of the country's ruin. The peasant's sheep brought forth lambs with white foreheads, and the lambs went to the lord in the name of righteousness. The sow farrowed pigs that went to the landlord's spit; the hen laid eggs and they went to his frying-pan; the cow dropped a male calf and it went to the landlord's herd; the mare foaled a horse foal and it went to make a saddle-horse for the lord; the peasant's wife had sons and they were used to look after the lord's property. At that point Miss Edgeworth ended her quotation from that 'curious specimen of Esthonian poetry,' restrained possibly by a virginal reticence from speculating too curiously on the interesting things that could happen to the peasant's daughters. She saw the obvious resemblance between Esthonian landlordism and Irish landlordism, but when she told, through the mouth of honest Thady Quirk, the tragic decline and fall of the Rackrents she saw the tragedy much more vividly in relation to the Rackrents and their doomed breed than in relation to the people they rackrented and the country that their way of living had pushed outwards to the black edge of ruin.

But William Carleton, looking through the eyes of Randy O'Rollick, the bailiff's son, saw the collapse of the Squanders of Castle Squander against a wide background. *Castle Rackrent* was Maria Edgeworth's best novel. *The Squanders of Castle Squander* was among the worst of Carleton's later, inferior works. For a considerable portion of its two red-backed volumes it drops all pretence of being a novel, changes into that treatise on the Irish land question that Barney Maglone, an admiring Ulster journalist, once suggested to Carleton that he should write. But even the portions of it untouched by statistics and quotations from learned reviews, sketch vividly enough the enormity of the whole breed, seed and generation of Irish landlordism. There was old Squire Squander whose amusements were hunting, shooting, steeple-chasing, and convivial debauchery. Every Christmas and Easter he whistled the hundredth psalm 'for he said that no man ought to pass through life without religion.' To unite himself properly with the aristocracy he married the daughter of Lord Mount Gallivant—against whom wise mothers locked their doors. She brought him no fortune, brought him only pride and a passion for expenditure to set the Squanders moving faster on the road to ruin. Wisdom came to them too late in the words of Uncle Tom Squander when he advised young Harry: 'Treat your tenants with kindness—with justice—remember that their toil, their cares, and their anxieties are all the source of your income. Remember they are men, and must feel a natural anxiety for the welfare and prosperity of their families; and that they have feelings as quick and affectionate, and, when need be, as indignant as your own . . . '

'And an excellent aim from behind a hedge,' said Harry, light-hearted before both death and imminent beggary, but, rank with the feeling of privilege, never quiet capable of realising that landlord and tenant were made of the same flesh and blood, that the prosperity of the landlord depended very closely on the prosperity of the tenant.

Harry Squander lived and died in the best tradition of the Rackrents and the Squanders who had between them a very representative selection of the bad qualities of Irish landlordism. Thady Quirk, speaking for Miss Edgeworth of Edgeworthstown, lamented the passing of the glory of the Rackrents, because, seen in relation to themselves and the domestic servants they maintained, the Rackrents had been powerful in the land and generous after a fashion. The big house was the biggest and loveliest thing that Thady the servant or Maria the lady had ever seen. But when William Carleton proposed—as he did at frequent and frequently dull intervals in his novels—solutions for the twisted problem of the ownership and use of Irish land, he was not, to his credit, thinking in terms of the big house. In the opening pages of *Valentine McClutchy*, in the series of letters between Hickman, the honest agent, and the profligate Lord Cumber, he laid bare as vividly and accurately as any man of his time the system that bled tenants to death in Ireland to make money to maintain an absentee landlord, losing heavily at cards, in London. In *The Emigrants of Ahadarra* he burdened the best of his novels with a careful, accurate historical estimate of the causes of hunger, evictions, emigration. Those problems were very important to him because they threatened the existence of his people, and the life of the country places in which he had experienced happiness.

He could hear always the words of Tom McMahon[1] returning from Dublin, coming again within sight of his old home, blessing the name of God because he had a home to return to, telling his son how his heart had longed for the sight of his own brave fields: 'for the lough there below, and the wild hills above us; for it wasn't until I was away from them that I felt how strong the love of them was in my heart.'

When he wrote those words, stabbing into the heart of the farmer of Ahadarra which was the heart of the people of Ireland, William Carleton was finally separated from his own green fields, from the lough and the wild hills. He was settled permanently in the city. It was not a very big city. In 1847, the year in which *The Emigrants of Ahadarra* was published in Belfast and London, and in which about seventy thousand of the Irish people died of hunger or famine

[1] *The Emigrants of Ahadarra*.

fever, and in which more than two hundred thousand emigrants sailed from Ireland as from a land accursed, the total population of Dublin was about two hundred and forty thousand. He lived for a while in the northern part of the city on the road that goes out through Clontarf and along the sea. His family began to grow up around him, and, in spite of a perpetual financial strain that was largely the result of his own bad management he was ideally happy with his family. Friends came to see him: notable people, because he also was gradually becoming a notable person. He was becoming so notable that English visitors came to see him. There is a story of one man from England who borrowed Carleton's dog and Carleton's gun in order to go shooting along the flat sands stretching northwards to Howth Head, looping like a friendly arm around the blue waters of Dublin bay. The Englishman shot valiantly and missed repeatedly until the exasperated dog, used to more accurate shooting, bit the visitor and trotted home to his master.

Later on Carleton lived in a prosperous part of the south side of the city. He became a familiar figure in Dublin, but he never really mixed in society, never held the place among urban people that he had once held among the simple people of the Clogher valley. His days of perpetual leaping and amazing weight-lifting were over, and to the people of Dublin, then as now, a man who wrote books was merely a man who wrote books. He lived a quiet life, the quietude disturbed only by the adventures of the literary man, by enthusiasms for new ideas, by occasional and transient enmities for other literary people, by quarrels with publishers, by meeting different people, intensely interesting as real people always are to the creative artist making his own world out of what his eyes see and his mind imagines of the world around him. He complained more than most men, lamenting generally the smallness of his purse. But his nearness to poverty was largely the result of his own foolish practice of selling copyrights; and he was granted a pension as the result of an appeal signed by most of the notables of the time. The Duke of Leinster signed it, along with a fairly representative collection of men with titles. The Provost of Trinity College signed it, and the President of Saint Patrick's College, Maynooth. Daniel Murray who was Catholic Archbishop of Dublin, signed it, and the Reverend Henry Montgomery and the Reverend Doctor Cooke. The presidents of learned institutions and equally learned societies signed it, and a large number of antiquaries, archaeologists, and men of medicine. Charles Gavan Duffy, the wisest of the Young Ireland men, signed it, and Colonel Blacker who wrote Orange ballads, and the son of Daniel O'Connell, and the father of Oscar Wilde, and Isaac Butt, and Maria Edgeworth who wrote from Edgeworthstown in the blackest year of Irish famine, considering that she was honouring her own name and the name of her father in testifying to the merits of William Carleton, interpreter of the Irish people.

And all the time the Irish people were dying miserably in cabins that stank to the skies with fever and the stench of putrid bodies, or dying in the ditches or on the desolate roads when the landlord's crowbar men had battered the cabins level with the ground, or passing out through the seaports on their way to new lands. He saw all this, for in Dublin he was never very far from the country, and in the streets of Dublin there was poverty and hunger, soup-kitchens, people selling souls and bodies for the sake of food. His own peevish, utterly unjustified complaints about the way in which Ireland neglected her greatest author, catch, as a radio catches atmospherics, something of the terrible, inevitable discontent of the time. In spite of these complaints he was possibly as happy as most men, happier than most on an island and among a people that some voices said were cursed by God.

TWELVE

HE MADE friends and he made enemies. He interpreted Ireland
in his own spasmodic uneven way; sometimes faultlessly reflecting
the sunshine, the green fields, echoing perfectly the birdsong, the
voices of little streams, the great unconquerable humour of the
people; sometimes hearing the thunder and painting the sky
darkening over acres black with decay; sometimes distributing abuse
and praise with a sincere, unsteady sort of regard for justice. After
a century the friendships and enmities do not seem so very important.
In the columns of the *Nation* he wrote an anonymous denunciation
of the 'flippant chat' of Charles Lever. Over the rights of the novel
Red Hall, later renamed *The Black Baronet*, he fought bitterly with
McGlashan, the publisher, whose mind anyway was weakening at
that time towards final and complete collapse. He visited London.
He met several English notables. He went walking in Wales. But
his few journeys and his not overwide contacts will, to-day, interest
only the occasional person prepared to listen quietly to the echoes
of the gossip of a dead time. His importance is that he gave life
without end to a vanishing, perishing people, saw something in
their souls, and in the outward manifestation of their spirit that
joins them solidly across the centuries to the people of this present
time. From the people that perished and the people that survived
he himself takes life wihout end.

It is his relation to the people of Ireland that makes important
his loose connection with the men of Young Ireland. The influence
of those young, idealistic revolutionaries had joined with the force
of his own genius, and with the power in his own people that
expressed itself in Denis O'Shaughnessy and Phelim O'Toole, to
rescue him from Caesar Otway and the New Reformation. He kept
telling them that he did not approve of their political principles,
by which he meant as likely as not that he disliked the revolutionary
separatism that ran like a strong current from Theobald Wolfe
Tone to Robert Emmet and John Mitchel. In later years he carried
this disapproval to the point of mocking and effective abuse. But
he approved of the Young Irelanders because apart from strong
statements, coming mostly from John Mitchel, against the abominations of English rule in Ireland, they had a better plan than most
for the internal reformation of the Irish people; not Caesar Otway's
reformation which began and ended with cursing the Pope and
the whore of Babylon, but a cultural, economic plan that would
lay the foundations for prosperous freedom. The plans of Young
Ireland may have included misprints and misspellings, but they

showed William Carleton, as wayward as the people to whom he belonged, the necessity for stability and reform. When he wrote *Valentine McClutchy* he was trying in his own way to teach and reform and remake.

At the great gathering of vagabonds that intruded into the *Squanders of Castle Squander* like a lost fragment from an old Gaelic satire, Bill-in-the-Bowl, who even in his legless condition was king of the vagabonds, pointed out that no man had a better right than himself to the office of Prime Minister in the proposed new Ireland. No matter what state of public feeling predominated, Bill could swivel around upon his bottom so as to face it very like a man and still more like a minister. His demands for public office ended all possibility of an *entente* between Bill's vagabonds and a party of young revolutionaries, whose words and aspirations were written down to parody the words and aspirations of Young Ireland; for Bill's men discovered that the young fellows wanted all available offices in the new order for their own benefit. 'And what are you to give us?' cried the tatterdemalions, symbolising suddenly the whole hungry Irish people.

"'Why,' replied the Young Ireland party, "have you no soul— no spirit for universal freedom? Have you no lofty aspirations?— no humanity?—no fire?—no lightning?—no thunder?"

"'No,' said Billy, "the devil a taste o' anything o' the kind we have stronger than brimstone; but what are you going to give us, if we officer you and commissariat you?'"

And when the young men with the aspirations promised the tatterdemalions Liberty, the swivelling, legless Billy, mindful of his own needs and the needs of his people, said they had as much liberty as they wanted and advised the revolutionary children to return to their books.

The most noticeable thing about Bill-in-the-Bowl was his lack of legs. The most noticeable thing about Ireland was, that with famine, fever, cholera and dysentery, the country was one general lazar-house. The objectionable feature of the bulk of Young Irelandism was to Carleton, that to the other miseries of the time it added a 'juvenile revolution.' He pointed out, with the irony of the Irish peasant surveying the antics of young gentlemen, that the government of the time were deeply indebted to the hopes and expectations of liberty stirred up in the people by Young Ireland. For with this glorious prospect of freedom before them how could men who sincerely loved their country think of dying of hunger? Didn't the young gentlemen practically go the length of maintaining that the Irishman that would dare to die in such a crisis was a traitor to his country and a slave to Lord John Russell who had had the potato-blight concocted in Downing Street deliberately to put the young gentlemen down?

But Carleton's denunciation of Young Ireland, or at least of the romantically revolutionary aspect of Young Ireland, was not governed noticeably by any steady, set political principle. He condemned 'the ferocious and brutal violence' of the language of John Mitchel who referred to Lord Clarendon as Butcher-General of Ireland, told Lord Clarendon that he expected no mercy from him, as, so help him God, he (Lord Clarendon) might expect none from him (Mitchel) should the revolutionary cause prosper. This, Carleton said, was not the language of common sense or common feeling, but of political insanity. But from Mitchel's point of view it was the only language possible under the circumstances: the people were dying; the mind of the nineteenth century exhibited in economic theory was responsible; so was the British government of Ireland, and the precariousness of the potato, and the callow selfishness of the landed classes. For an honest courageous man, whose temperament and whose prose-style had come under the influence of Thomas Carlyle, but who acted where Carlyle growled in prophetic self-satisfaction, the only thing to do was stand up before all men and speak the truth. John Mitchel did that, first in the *Nation*, later more inflammably in the *United Irishman*, later in the dock when a carefully-selected jury sent him overseas for life. He thought quite sensibly that no trade regulations and no unalterable economic laws should be allowed to take food out of Ireland while the people of Ireland died of hunger. He thought quite sensibly that if men had to die at all they should die like men, not like the plants that rotted around them in the fields. They should fight for food. They should tear down the whole structure that had brought them to such misery.

It was a wild, anarchic message, but it was spoken in the middle of anarchy. It was a million miles away from the rosy revolution that looked forward to liberty and the world's great age beginning anew and the golden time returning. It was in another world from 'Speranza', the mother of Oscar Wilde, writing in the last number of the *Nation* published previous to its suppression, her famous laughable incitement to rebellion: 'Gather round the standard of your chiefs. Who dares to say he will not follow, when O'Brien leads? Or who amongst you is so abject that he will grovel in the squalid misery of his hut, or be content to be flung from the ditch side into the living tomb of the poorhouse, rather than charge proudly like brave men and free men, with that glorious young Meagher at their head, upon the hired mercenaries of their enemies? One bold, one decisive move. One instant to take breath, and then a rising—a rush, a charge from the north, south, east, and west, upon the English garrison, and *the land is ours*. Do your eyes flash—do your hearts throb at the prospect of having *a country*?'

This was part of the 'torrent of patriotic ink' that he condemned wisely enough in the *Nation*. Inspired by that patriotism were the 'clubs with antiquated and unpronounceable names formed by all the young lads of Dublin, each with its juvenile president who boldly pronounced the memorised war-speech.' The young fellow was 'no true herokin who did not wear a silver pike in his breast to show the world the dreadful tenor of his patriotism,' and, 'a vast number of terrible pikes were furnished to them by the detectives, who in general drilled them first and afterwards reported them to the government.' Then after the 1848 revolution in France there were wild words in Dublin about the possibilities of the barricades. 'Old bottles rose three farthings a hundred; and some of the dealers in old glass are still anxious for another outbreak.' And when William Smith O'Brien, glorious in his top hat, his ideals, his lineage, did lead out a few countrymen to rebellion in a remote part of Munster they went 'without money, without men, without food, without discipline, officers, arms, or ammunition, in the glowing heat of their valour—big with the hopes of a successful revolution, for the accomplishing of which they were so admirably provided—they attacked a police barrack, and were defeated in a cabbage garden.'[1]

It was and is still easily possible for some Irishmen to indulge in this type of foolery and, incidentally, to provide uproarious amusement for other Irishmen. But it would be wrong to confuse the foolery with the occasional moments of practical revolution, to forget that both the foolery and the practical revolution were acting as rough indicators of the unrest and disorder in Irish politics. He was temperamentally incapable of going wholeheartedly into any of the movements of his time, or of accepting any other man's solution for the complicated problems of his country. The great O'Connell stood damned in Carleton's eyes as an agitator, and because of agitators he held that the moral character of the people was degenerating. But the sober truth was that few men had done more than O'Connell to raise the people from baseness and beggary to something of integrity and self-reliance.

The great political issue of Carleton's time and of the whole nineteenth century was the repeated attempt to repeal the Act of Union, to give Ireland its own independent parliament. He knew enough of history to know that during his own childhood men had scandalously acquired wealth and titles by the simple process of

[1] *The Squanders of Castle Squander*, vol. ii.

smiling at Lord Castlereagh and voting solid for the Legislative Union of Great Britain and Ireland. Tom Topertoe who became Lord Castle Cumber had 'the high honour of being a union lord—that is to say, his attachment to his principles was so steady, that he did not hesitate to sell his country for a title, and something besides.' There was not to be found 'in the annals of all history, any political negotiation based upon such rank and festering corruption as was the Legislative Union.'[1]

But William Carleton never knew enough about these things, never kept his two feet in the same place long enough, to find for himself a stable, logical approach to the central political problem that had so much to do with the chaos of the Irish nineteenth century. In one place he makes a character say sententiously: 'If Ireland is to have her own parliament it will not be got by force of arms, but by the force of public opinion.'[2] When the *Dublin Evening Mail* devoted a leading article[3] to attacking him, on grounds both literary and political as an unworthy holder of a civil list pension, he defended himself in a letter, never published in that newspaper, defining reasonably well his own position towards politics: 'I am not now nor have I ever been at any time a Repealer. I am not a Young Irelander, nor, in a political sense at least, an old one. I am no Republican, no Jacobin, no Communist, but a plain, retiring literary man who wishes to avoid politics, and to devote his future life to such works as he hopes may improve his country and elevate her people.'[4] In one place he points out that the Orange jingle 'Lillibullero' was the most pointless and stupid production that ever came from the brain of man.[5] In another place he could write that 'a greater curse could not be inflicted on the country than to give it a parliament of its own making,' falling back on the Orange argument, ever old and ever new and never quite justified, that after Repeal the Catholic priesthood would become a formidable body of politicians with no interest but that of their own Church.

There were a few contradictions here. But neither in William Carleton nor in the country and period in which he lived should the discovery of contradictions cause surprise. Yet he would have agreed roughly with the advice that Lever in *Luttrell of Aran* made Luttrell give to Vyner, the Englishman about to become a property-owner in an out-of-the-way part of Donegal. Luttrell wanted to know what Vyner would do with the land, for the people who lived there would scarcely ever allow him to assert a single right of property. If he

1 O'Donoghue, vol. ii.
2 *The Red-Haired Man's Wife.*
3 July 3, 1848.
4 O'Donoghue, vol. ii.
5 *Willy Reilly.*

stocked it with sheep and sent an agent, they would eat the mutton and shoot the agent. To appeal to the law would be as effective as threatening a New Zealander with a bill in Chancery; and if Vyner himself came to live on his property he would be shot at when prices rose and the nights grew longer. For Ireland was not to be bettered by men like Vyner. 'It is out of our own rough energies must come the cure for our own coarse maladies.'

Lever discovered that wisdom in the intervals of the 'flippant chat' with which he filled volume after volume; and, in spite of foolish talk of war and wild talk of liberty, the men of Young Ireland had a fairly steady grasp on a stick capable of prodding those energies into life. Their poets romanticised and glorified the past. Mangan saw visions of the lost glories of the once proud people of Banba and walked entranced through a land of bright sunshine and perpetual morning in the days of the great King of the West, Cathal Mor of the Wine-red hand. That appeal to the past is recurrent in the story of modern Ireland. It can lead to vapourings and delusions. It can also have a beneficial strengthening effect on the present. In the days of Young Ireland it did not prevent Thomas Davis from writing sensibly about Sir Robert Kane's book *The Industrial Resources of Ireland*. (Lever, after a restless night in an inn in Connaught, said that flea-hunting could give employment to the population of one province.) The blinding and frequently ersatz radiance of the past did not prevent the writers in the *Nation* from drawing up a rough draft of a plan for economic and cultural and social reform; and on many of the points in that plan William Carleton sensibly submitted to their influence.

Their influence was strengthened by his candid appreciation of their high character. He wrote: 'It is due to them to say, however, that apart from their folly as politicians, it would be impossible to find a more highminded and honourable set of men; but by far the ablest among them was Gavan Duffy.'

But it was for Thomas Osborne Davis that William Carleton reserved the highest, most sincere tribute he ever paid to any man, proving once again the extraordinary personality that was lost somewhere in mediocre poems and patriotic ballads and quiet, thoughtful essays. Davis drew to himself and held under his influence all that was best in the Ireland of his time; and, fresh from the sorrow of that burial scene in Mount Jerome, Carleton wrote of 'inexorable death that in the course of one short and disastrous week extinguished that spirit, to whose pure lustre the eyes of our country would have one day turned as to a leading star.'[1] He made one of the best attempts that has been made to analyse the reasons why men of

1 Preface to *Parra Sastha* or *The History of Paddy-Go-Easy and his wife, Nancy*.

differing types were variously attracted to Davis. He had 'a character so full and complete, a mind so large and comprehensive.' He was 'not only a man of genius, but a man of genius without the shadow of those errors, which almost always accompany it,' and to the wonderful and varied powers of his intellect, and the purity and strength of his principle, and the ever-living truth which kindled all his purposes, he added the spell of a child-like and loving heart, 'As a poet, he could have sung a people into freedom; as a statesman, he had capacity to deal with empires; in the field he would have led armies; in the council, he would have balanced and guided the destiny of nations.' The heart of Thomas Davis, wrote William Carleton, was as pure and as easily touched as the drop of dew on the blade of grass; and his society and conversation made you a better man; and 'his brief life and appearance here were not a thing of ordinary being, but a miracle and a mystery.' The love of Thomas Davis for the traditional music of Ireland very naturally appealed to a man who had heard his mother sing with all the gathered sweetness of the centuries; and, over that premature grave, William Carleton thought: 'That he was my friend is at once my pride and my sorrow. Only on one question did we differ.'

A sceptical present-day Irishman reading the poems and prose of Thomas Davis might wonder what all the eulogy was about, might wonder, also, had Carleton's heart been too deeply affected by the sad burial of one who died young. But all the men of that time who had occasion to speak of Davis spoke of him in that same high language of praise, and on succeeding generations his influence has been out of all proportion to the length of his life or any sceptical estimate of the importance of his work. The devil himself could not doubt that Carleton had been deeply influenced by Davis, by the men who gathered around Davis while he lived, whose mourning for him when dead began the perpetuation of his memory. From no other living man could Carleton have said that he differed only on one point; and his close agreement with Thomas Davis brings him directly into the line of the men who down through that century worked, sometimes wisely and sometimes foolishly, to make order out of chaos.

He approached his own portion of that work of formation like the careful wife of a poor farmer preparing to clean up the house. His people, his own beloved people, the grandest peasantry on earth and all that, could be, and often were, dirty, disorderly and drunken. Under the auspices of Young Ireland he decided to do something about it.

THIRTEEN

ACTUALLY he wrote very little, only a few essays for the newspaper called the *Nation*. But after *Valentine McClutchy* he felt with stiffening conviction that he must continue to be something more than the student of character or the careful recorder of words and deeds. When Davis died in the fall of 1845 he was working on a short life of Wolfe Tone, for publication in Duffy's *Library of Ireland* a series of small, prayer-book-format volumes definitely designed to educate and improve the Irish people. Carleton was asked to do something to keep the series going and after nine days' work filled the gap with the story of *Parra Sastha* or *Paddy-Go-Easy and his wife, Nancy*. He probably saw the rich humour of substituting for the life-story of an adventurer and doctrinaire patriot, with all his gallantry and Gallic dash, imposing on the Irish people a green-white-and-gold variation on the theme of the French tricolour, a study of a lazy, dirty farmer reformed to cleanliness by the efforts of his energetic wife. Unfortunately a considerable proportion of his Irish readers didn't see the joke, didn't see the point of the allegory in which Paddy and Nancy were the two halves of the soul of Ireland. The little book gave offence, was interpreted as a betrayal of Ireland into the hands of the base and bloody Saxons who delighted in jeers and gibes about the dirty Irish. That was, and is, a not uncommon Irish reaction to criticism of Irish failings. It was, anyway, very easy, the more so because the argument had strong justification, to blame the dirt, and everything else that was unpleasant, on Irish landlordism and English misrule.

But William Carleton was not an English tourist, spending fourteen days in Ireland like a man spending fourteen days in a dungeon, taking back in his mind a confused vision of pigs playing and dung-heaps steaming beside the mud-hovels. William Carleton knew his own people, the clean and the dirty, the well-kept houses and the ill-kept houses. He knew also how tenants on estates were afraid to keep clean houses in case the landlord or his agent or his agent's agent would see cleanliness and assume prosperity and automatically raise the rent. He had nothing to gain from libelling his own people. If he detailed the dirt of Paddy in his farmhouse, he detailed also the careless, drunken extravagance of the Squanders in their decaying mansion. Because he loved Paddy in spite of all his failings, because he belonged to the people that Paddy represented, because deep in his own soul was the chaotic, untidy soul of Paddy, he brought him salvation in the neat form and deft hands of Nancy. For the Squanders there could obviously be no salvation.

Dinny Delap, the neighbours said, roaring with honest laughter, had gone and got himself an iron plough. Dinny from over the river, little Dinny with the cast in his eye, the same dirty little scrub that had the nerve to laugh at a better man than himself for harrowing his oats with a thorn bush and a stone laid on top of it, Dinny hadn't been content to do as his neighbours did and put up with a wooden plough. Loudest among the laughers was the great breed of Go-Easies, each man content to do as his father had done before him; and greatest among the Go-Easies was Paddy, the heir to the place, content to dress as his father before him had dressed, content to keep the place as the place always had been. Paddy smoked his father's pipe, wore the frieze coat that his father had worn, and no two parts of his clothes were either good or bad at the same time.

In the tottering Go-Easy farmhouse the nose was gratified by a very heterogeneous odour, compounded of various villainous smells, among which predominated the smell of stale chamberlye and rotten buttermilk, garnished with a strong tincture of the heavy and sickening exhalation of greasy wool kept in a close place. The churn used by Paddy's sisters was 'constantly covered inside with the old undisturbed wreck of buttermilk.' The wooden settle was unhinged. The chairs creaked 'musically'. The table would have creaked but for the lubricating effect of dirt. The pot in which they cooked wanted an ear. The dust on the floor was swept into the holes. The lid was gone from the salt-box and inside there was salt and soot. The mealchests were broken and burrowed by mice; and Paddy's sisters slept in the loft with the wool-fleeces.

The purpose of allegory cries out for exaggeration, and William Carleton spared no detail. Possibly nowhere in the wide world was there any place as dirty as he made the house and farm of poor, pipe-sucking, good-natured, ancestor-worshipping Paddy. In the filthy farmyard the pig lay 'in the black, sludgy filth, his belly to the sun, his small sensual eyes shut with an expression of luxurious enjoyment that would shame an alderman.' The thatch of the out-houses was gone and useless straw lay rotting in the haggard where the staggering stacks leaned crazily against each other. In the car-house there were no cars; they lay out exposed to the weather, one of them blocking a gap into a field. Bony horses and bony cattle grazed greedily, their hips clotted with tartles of dung. The doors of the outhouses were tied up with rope, excepting the door of the barn which swung crazily on one hinge. The farm began with 'a late field of oats or rather of docks and thistles, colt's foot and presha, among which a keen eye might discern something in the shape of oats.' Since his father and grandfather had never cultivated head-ridges because it was considered 'mane' to do so, Paddy, strong in his respect for the past, scorned 'to go beyant them.' The fields were dirty and the drains were dirty, 'the sheep were dirty, the cows were dirty, the horses were dirty; and, to crown all, Paddy himself was dirty.'

All this detailed description of dirt, all the humorous dialogue of the story, must have meant nine days of lively writing; too lively for many of his less realistic readers, unable to see that an essay on Irish dirt was one effective way of giving Irish cleanliness a fighting chance. James Duffy, the publisher, felt that the good reputation of the series in which the book was published had betrayed him into handling something offensive to his public and ruinous to his own good name. But with the odd honesty of the man, who knew anyway that he had done nothing worse than accumulate on one farm displeasing things that he had seen in various places, Carleton 'affectionately and respectfully' dedicated the little book to the people of Ireland as a 'feeble attempt to communicate to them information designed to improve their condition and add to their information and comfort.' If the perusal of its pages succeeded in banishing the 'habits of indolence and want of cleanliness' that he had satirised he would feel that he had been the humble means of rendering an important service to his country. His object had been 'to inculcate habits of industry, punctuality, cleanliness, comfort, intelligence, and that principle of social progress which the landlords of Ireland have never or seldom made any earnest attempt to develop among their tenantry.'

But in spite of the dedication, in spite of the patently laudable intention, William Carleton had managed to jump with both feet on one of those peculiar paradoxical intolerancies of the more nationally-minded minority of the most tolerant people on God's earth. That minority abused the book. The majority, apparently, displayed that tolerance in purchasing it; and later editions gave him the opportunity of apologising for any past offensiveness. 'In drawing Paddy as the representative of a certain class,' he wrote, 'we beg the reader to understand that that class, so far from constituting the majority of our countrymen, is only intended to comprise within it a certain section of them; but, still, a section more numerous than it ought to be, and sufficient, in consequence, to impress an unfavourable character upon the country at large.'

He could and did defend himself by pointing out that, if he had held up Paddy as a scarecrow he had held up his wife as an example. The place of Nancy in the allegory was to represent 'our national activity, and the awakened tendencies to progress and improvement.' She came into the life of Paddy and his sisters with new ideas, new methods, a love of cleanliness and order, and the discreet power to

112

soften the censure against their want of cleanliness that her suggestions and corrections implied. Those suggestions and corrections would sound absolutely correct from the lips of any careful Irish country-woman, faced with the problem of bringing order and cleanliness where only dirt and disorder had been. 'Where there are so many cows,' she told the girls, with a certain acid gentleness, 'surely one butter-milk tub or one churn is not enough, an' that I suppose is the raison why the vessels have a sour and sickenin' smell, and why the butther' turned out so badly, an' the milk so dangerous to taste. Now, if you had two churns all along, so as that you could scald one of them with boiling water, and dry it out in the open air, you'd have very different milk an' butther from what you have. If the milk vessels are well washed, kept sweet an' clean, your milk and butther will be sweet and clean; so now we mark Paddy down for a new set of milk vessels, churn and all, don't we girls?'

That was all as delightfully practical as the hints he borrowed from Martin Doyle's 'admirable little work', *Hints to the Small Farmers of the County of Wexford,* and published as an appendix to the story of Paddy and Nancy. The appendix bristled with observations on the condition and quality of land, preparation of the soil, cottage cleanliness, prudence and sobriety and industry, on the care to be taken in giving clover to cows, on the cutting and planting of potatoes, the sowing of turnips and the pickling of wheat, on manures and marl and irrigation. It told how dairies should be kept and quoted Wilkinson's 'excellent marks by which every one may soon learn how to choose his cow.' The marks were given in rhyme that detailed the qualities of the desirable cow:

> *'She's long in her face, she's fine in her horn,*
> *She'll quickly get fat without cake or corn;*
> *She's clear in her jaws, she's full in her chine*
> *She's heavy in flank and wide in her loin.'*

The existence and acceptance of Martin Doyle's book showed that even under the shadow of famine, in defiance of landlordism and insecurity of tenure and rents that perpetually kept rising, the native love of thrift and the desire for improvement to which the book appealed had obstinately refused to perish; and if the touchy patriots who roared because a man said that dirt was not unknown in Ireland had only prayed God for intelligence and re-read with care the story of Paddy-Go-Easy they would have found there the most inspiring message of hope written in that terrible time. It was not the hope of the golden age returning, or the world beginning anew through the rant of 'Speranza' or Meagher of the Sword,

113

or the codology of William Smith O'Brien. It was the simple, sensible statement that the dirty could become clean and the slothful become industrious, that through industry could come a stiffening of the backbone, a hardening of the muscles. For the success of Nancy's reformation posited good-nature in Paddy and his sisters, ability to take correction, a subconscious desire after better things. The allegory could reach out to include every aspect of the disordered life of the Irish people.

When Nancy's work was done, everything in the kitchen was white and clean and in its place. The floor was 'level as a lake and beautifully tiled,' the large settle as white as milk, the dresser equipped with its shining array of wood and delf and pewter. The spacious chimney-brace was abundantly stored with huge sides of fat, yellow bacon and darker masses of hung beef. 'Of a summer evening, nothing could be more delightful than to see that spacious and beautiful kitchen lit up by the golden beams of the cloudless sun as they shone in large amber shafts through the windows, filling the whole place with light, cheerfulness and enjoyment.' Below the kitchen was the boarded parlour becomingly furnished, the bedrooms redolent of sweet-scented herbs.

It was, maybe, his memory of boyhood in the valley. It was also his hope for rural Ireland in the coming time, a land of peace and plenty and security, a land no longer divided against itself, no longer dumb with the weight of overhanging shadow. It was the peasant's vision of the golden age.

A Capuchin friar in the city of Cork had decided in the name of God to make the Irish a sober people, and, acting as an interesting parallel to O'Connell's mass-meetings, and contributing largely to the remarkable orderliness among O'Connell's audiences, were Father Theobald Mathew's mass-meetings. Sober people took the pledge to remain sober. Drinkers decided to drink no more. Drunkards decided to make complete reformation. Dipsomaniacs recovered their lost manhood. Daniel O'Connell admired Father Mathew. Thomas Carlyle admired him. The whole world admired him. Publicans, brewers and distillers—with a certain amount of understandable reluctance—admired him. Anyway, as far as Ireland was concerned, the people hardest hit by the friar's campaign for sobriety were not the licensed publicans, brewers and distillers. In the ten years between 1820 and 1830 the recorded increase in the Irish consumption of spirits was six million gallons. In 1828 the drinking recorded by official figures was about ten million gallons, but the story told by official figures would have left rural Ireland still roaring with the thirst. A parliamentary committee enquiring into the matter in 1834 stated dolefully that 'even in the most civilised districts of Ulster private distillation has prevailed very extensively for some time past.'

Private distillation was parliamentary language for poteen, white and potent and flavoured slightly with the smell of turf-smoke, from one point of view about the only social amenity left to the people of the cabins. But from Father Mathew's point of view, which was really the more social point of view, poteen was an exceedingly dangerous playmate, an exceedingly tyrannical master. He was the model of the sensible temperance reformer, following the cheerful road of reason between bees in the bonnet and pink rats on the ceiling. Beyond a doubt the extremely sodden condition of the people of Ireland cried out for vigorous words and extreme actions. The support of every man and woman who, apart altogether from temperance faddists, wanted to see the revival of the people was genuinely behind that remarkable friar. Maria Edgeworth was behind him when she wrote the story *Orlandino*. William Carleton was behind him when he wrote *Art Maguire* or *The Broken Pledge*.

It was not a great story. It followed faithfully enough the vagaries of a conceited young man determined or doomed to drink himself to death. But it had no artistic intensity, none of the insight into the mind of a man enslaved by the bottle that makes remarkable a book like *The Lost Weekend*. It had little of Carleton's native fun, little of his vivid eye for character. It was a moral tract in black-and-white tones, comically notable because it revealed the writer once again with a leg swinging on either side of the fence, because it exposed him again to the thunders of his critics. There was a great deal to be said for the Cork Capuchin who preached temperance. There was also a great deal to be said for poteen and, in various places, both before and after the telling of the story of Art Maguire, William Carleton said it.

At Finglas village on the road into Dublin, Barney Branagan[1] had looked ahead, his heart warming as he saw the sign over the hospitable door of the Saint Patrick public-house. The right hand of the saint was extended perpetually towards the thirsty traveller and on his jolly face was cordial and friendly welcome. The sign showed, as background to the picture of the saint, two men sitting at a table and feeding night and day upon beef and strong ale 'whilst the bluff and good-humoured patron of conviviality instead of a pitiful tape and medal, held a substantial crozier in his hand, with which he was ready to drive any creeping snake-like sinner out of the house, who denied his authority and refused to take his liquor.' For in the days of Barney Branagan it was 'Father Patrick, and not Father Mathew who bore the palm.' Nor was the 'watery Corkonian'

---

[1] *The Clarionet, The Dead Boxer, Barney Branagan*, published in one volume in 1850.

to imagine that the saint would fail in re-establishing the principles to which at Finglas he had so long given the support of his crozier and his countenance.

The healthy Chestertonian approach to the bottle and glass and little brown jug was sensible and rational and would have been readily understood by Father Mathew. Nor was there any reason why a man who praised the virtues of poteen could not also praise the virtues of temperance. But the contradiction was too obvious to be passed over by those who had grown accustomed to finding contradictions in the behaviour of William Carleton and there were even uncharitable people ready to suggest that the patently sincere little tract about the decline and fall of Art Maguire was written with the tongue in the cheek. But quite sincerely he dedicated the little book to Father Mathew as 'the providential instrument of producing among his countrymen the most wonderful and salutary change that has ever been recorded in the moral history of man.' In a private letter to the friar, among the many conventional phrases essential to a letter of that type, he emphasised his wish to see his countrymen rescued 'from the influence of a habit that has proved itself such a multiplied and many-shaped curse to their health, their industry, and their morals.' Knowing that in more matters than his predilection for whisky punch he had made himself appear to the Catholic majority as a peculiar propagandist for any movement founded by a Catholic friar, he went out of his way in a preface to soothe the suspicions of those who felt 'apprehensive that anything calculated to injure the doctrinal convictions of the Catholic people might be suffered to creep into these tales.' What he wanted to do was through the instrumentality of 'truthful fiction' to act on the feelings of his fellow-countrymen and furnish them with a 'pleasing encyclopaedia of social duty.'

It is by no means the most colourful chapter in his writings. The moral maxims look dull enough when balanced against the randy rhymes and boisterous eulogies in which he praised the strong warmth of Irish whisky. 'Poteen when taken neat,' roared Randy O'Rollick, 'beats champagne all to nothing in rapidity of operation.' The staged and arranged incidents in the story of Art Maguire are deader than death when compared with all the wild tales of stillers in the mountains and gaugers outwitted in which his great memory and imagination took delight. The hiding-place of the illicit distiller like the underground schoolroom of the hedge-schoolmaster was one of the strong social institutions of a broken people whose very minds moved underground, whose souls were in hiding. It would have been easy to leave the people in peace with the white water that brought temporary forgetfulness. But this man who had, himself, so much to remember and so much to forget had also in common with the people to whom he belonged a native feeling for order as the basis of strength and dignity.

Father Mathew's great campaign, he pointed out, was a credit to more than Father Mathew, for deep down in the people there was something that responded to the appeal to be strong and decent and 'it was unquestionable that had the religious and moral feelings of the Irish people been neglected (by the priests) the principle of temperance would never have taken such deep root in the heart of the nation.' Across the sea Thomas Carlyle, with a complacency that, because the man had no manners, was generally mistaken for prophetic discontent, was assuring the people of England, Scotland and Wales that deep down within them they had the divine something that would yet unseat Plugson of Undershot, and remake the world. It was easy enough feeling that way in Chelsea. But it was very easy to fail to see anything good in a people that had nothing but rags, tottering mud walls, the horror of a great hunger. Watching a nation die it was so easy to lose hope. Yet William Carleton who lost so many valuable things never lost that hope in his own people that is the abiding mark of the great democrat.

Characteristically, he could take back with one hand the laurels he gave with the other, not because of dishonesty or double-dealing, but because no counsel of common sense could stop his attempts to define the exact outline between what he felt to be right and what he felt to be wrong. His mind was never made for the exact work of defining and drawing outlines and making nice distinctions. At one moment he could praise the priests of Ireland because their work in the hearts of the Irish people made possible the success of Father Mathew. At another moment he could say that the priests had not made proper and complete use of 'either their sacerdotal privileges, or the ecclesiastical machinery within their reach' to aid in the suppression of Irish crime. If the priests, he said, were as anxious to suppress crime as they were to repeal the Act of Union or to sustain the Conciliation Hall exchequer 'at the expense of a naked, perishing and famine-struck people' then the whole country 'would not be steeped in crime as it is, nor disgraceful to the religion which its perpetrators profess.' But even while making the accusation he had an uneasy foreboding of the criticism it might provoke, and attempted to build up his fortifications before the attack by stating that not for one moment did he believe that the priests directly encouraged crime, for: 'in one point of view we must unhesitatingly grant, that the Catholic priesthood of Ireland are an example to the priesthood of any other church or religion in the world. In the administration of their rites and sacraments at the bed of death and sickness—in the mountain hut, in the house of the wealthy farmer, in the pest-house, in the hospital and fever *bohog,* on the side of the public road—they are ever to be found at their post nobly discharging their duties.'[1]

No analytical method, unless aided by special insight or intuition, could draw from that particular passage what exactly William Carleton did feel that the priests could have done to prevent a people in torment from doing the violent deeds of the tormented. On the same page, in one stilted sentence, he increases the complication by showing his clear consciousness that neither the priests nor the people were ultimately responsible for the ground current of blood and violence sweeping along under the life of Ireland in the nineteenth century. He wrote: 'In every country whose political, commercial, or social relations, are not properly settled, or in which there exists a struggle between the principles at variance with civil order and those of enlightened progress, there will always be found a considerable portion of the population ripe and ready for violence and crime.'

John Mitchel, for all his 'political insanity', had the type of mind that immediately clarified a situation by reducing it to its elements, and one page of his violent words can be infinitely more illuminating than all Carleton's efforts to be abstract and detached, to lay the exact amount of praise and blame exactly where each belonged. Mitchel saw clearly enough that the killing of odious landlords, agents, tithe proctors and bailiffs had certainly been dreadful atrocities, but the country people of Ireland had regarded them not as murders but as executions. There was no law on either side but, as Mitchel saw it, 'more substantial justice, on the whole, is done by the "midnight legislators" than by the judges of Assize.' Because of his own temperament and his memories of first enthusiasm for Thomas Carlyle, Mitchel to the end of his days had no liking for the methods of secret and oath-bound societies. Ribbonism had secrecy and the swearing of oaths, and was, as well, spasmodic and unorganised both in particular action and in general outline. But for Mitchel it had the merit of being a flat negation of British law in Ireland, 'a great manufactory of disaffection and rebellion, and one which the government will never be able to reach.' In other words, Ribbonism—a name that meant nothing more clearly defined than discontent expressing itself in violence—kept the fires of rebellion burning until the time and the man would come to fan them into one universal conflagration. No government could effectively smother those fires, for they burned secretly in the hearts of men resenting injustice. Although the violent expression of that resentment could be foolish and terrible, could go awry and destroy the innocent with the guilty, could be twisted to evil purposes by evil men,

[1] *The Tithe Proctor.*

yet it is on the survival in the human heart of that primitive anger at wrong and tyranny that the cause of freedom must ultimately depend.

The mental process that led the Irish countryman into the ranks of the Whiteboys was well enough described by Michael Banim in the story *Crohoore of the Bill-Hook,* when a poor man called Dermid decides, after suffering increasing exactions from collectors of tithes and collectors of rent, that there is no law or mercy in the land for the papist or the poor. Then Dermid: 'continued his long walk, chewing the ever-rising cud of this bitter, and desperate, and obstinate thought; he brought to mind at the same time, all the life's labour and sweat he had uselessly expended; he crossed the threshold of his puddled hovel, and heard his children squalling for food; and then he turned his back on them; walked hastily abroad; gave a kick to the idle spade he met on his way; sought out some dozen Dermids or Paddies similarly situated with himself; between them they agreed to take the tithe-proctors and the law of tithes into their own hands; proposed silly oaths to each other; and the result was "the boys" . . . called, apart from the abbreviation, Whiteboys.'

That was Whiteboyism. That was something that ran in all Irish secret societies, and William Carleton knew it as well as Michael Banim or John Mitchel or anybody else in Ireland. He knew the mixture of motives that brought men together by night, swearing terrible oaths, burning and destroying property, taking human lives. He knew the resentment against tithe-proctors and rack-renting landlords. He knew the bitter sectarian hatreds that cracked the life of parts of the country into night-war between rival secret societies. In his youth he had taken the oath in one of these societies, and he knew how young men, unembittered by any grievance, could still be led into the dangerous business through idleness or frivolity or dare-devilry. He knew also that it could at times suit the purposes of high government to develop these conspiracies by specially chosen agents; and when he wrote *Rody the Rover* or *The Ribbonman* he was absorbed by that aspect of the business to the exclusion of everything else.

The villainous Rody, a wandering *agent provocateur,* brought ruin and destruction to the prosperous village of Ballybracken, made unwontedly prosperous so as to heighten by force of contrast the reader's sense of the misery that followed plotting and violence. Only to an old tramp called Tickling Tony did Rody reveal the purpose of his presence in Ballybracken, describing himself as an emissary or 'a person that is sent out to do a particular thing.' When Tickling Tony, acting rather obviously to gather information for the sake of the reader, questioned Rody as to what general end he had in view, the emissary answered: 'What object? Why, is it nothing to be able to say that the Irish are a disaffected, riotous, unscrupulous and blood-thirsty people, whom common laws cannot restrain? Is it nothing to give the country a bad name . . .?' Rody's method of provoking a conspiracy and then betraying the conspirators to gaol, the gallows, or transportation, showed that William Carleton was aware of the methods of secret police as an attack on the liberties of the people. Rody himself proudly boasted that: 'the origin of this conspiracy against the people will not be easily come at . . . because it seems to clothe itself with the prejudices of the people themselves. How then can they suspect it to be unfriendly to their own interests?'

Carleton never came closer to a sordid acceptance of the many miseries of his time than in the little book in which he told the story of Rody the Rover, meaning that story to act as a warning to his people against the work of scoundrels like Rody and in general, as a warning against conspiracy and lawless violence. For the village of Ballybracken there was no happy ending, as there had been for the townland of Ahadarra. The prosperity of the place was gone. An innocent young man was hanged, an innocent girl seduced, an old couple left to broken-hearted death. He never came nearer to sedition than when he traced through the pages of that book the links of the chain that bound Rody the Rover to the government in Dublin Castle, stating plainly that: 'government was certainly under serious obligations to Rody the Rover.' Yet the book was unpopular with young men who were genuine revolutionaries, because they detected there a tendency to regard even genuine revolutionaries as *agents provocateurs*. In detecting that tendency they were not greatly mistaken.

For William Carleton was a peasant who became a novelist and did his best to be a reformer. He could never, like Mitchel, the gentleman who became a revolutionary, welcome murder as a weapon against murder, and disorder from below as the only answer to disorder imposed from above. In that he was much less logical than Mitchel and the whole revolutionary Ireland and revolutionary Europe of which Mitchel was a part. But he was much more human, in the sense in which it is human to be torn with pity for the sorrows of poor people. The logical revolutionary who accepts the necessity of violence as a weapon against violence can be correct and wise in his own environment, but he has one foot on the road to the cell in which Ivanov, the official in Arthur Koestler's *Darkness at Noon,* tells his prisoner: 'I have not a spark of pity . . . the vice of pity I have up till now managed to avoid. The smallest dose of it and you are lost.'

More than one hundred years before the madness of the modern logical revolutionary William Carleton walked in a troubled time across the flat green land of Louth on the eastern shore of Ireland. He saw the body of Paddy Devaun high on the gallows at the cross-roads of Corcreagh, heard the story of Paddy Devaun's mother, crossing and recrossing her own threshold, looking up at that hideous swinging object, mourning her poor martyr of a son. The terrible picture was painted forever in his mind, and looking out over Ireland he could always see in vision the sorrowful homes into which violence had brought loneliness and death. It was weak and illogical, things being as they were, to suppose that submission to injustice could ever bring peace. But then William Carleton was seldom anything but illogical; and because his great heart was large enough, in spite of his erratic head, to find room for all the people of Ireland, he sorrowed with the sorrowing mothers mourning the bravery and the foolishness of their sons.

FOURTEEN

It was the great event in the life-time of William Carleton. It was the black cloud coming up to fill the bluest sky, casting the shadow of death over the green fields. It was the sharp test for the nineteenth century, the challenge to ships and mines and machinery and talk of progress and Macaulay prophesying a new Manchester in the wilds of Connemara; and the nineteenth century failed as every age in human history has failed before its bitterest trials, failed because it was not even aware that its ideas and its material resources had been challenged. The challenge came from death, and, in Ireland, not many miles from Manchester thousands of men and women and children died horribly in the course of a few years. The challenge came from hunger and in 1836, a year not even catalogued as a year of famine, out of the eight million people in Ireland two-and-a-half millions were on the edge of starvation. When William Carleton died, a little more than thirty years later, the population of the country had shrunk to a little over five millions. They had died of hunger and fever, in squalid huts, in overcrowded workhouses, in fields, in ditches, along the open roads. They had sailed westwards over the sea looking for new lands and new lives, and famine and fever had followed them over the water. On the ship *Erin Queen* 493 people sailed and 136 died on the voyage; on the *Avon* 552 sailed and 246 died; on the *Virginia* 476 sailed and 267 died; on another ship 600 sailed and 500 died. Famine and fever followed them to other lands and in unmarked and unknown graves hundreds found their only possible peace.

But figures mean nothing. A nation came very close to total extinction and figures can say only that so many died, so many emigrated, so many survived; that there was this or that reason in the laws of trade and economics for death and emigration and survival. But William Carleton belonged to the Irish people, understood the Irish people. He was, through all the years after his marriage, a literary man living an unadventurous life. But he saw all the horror; and deep within him, in the soul of the boy who know the suffering people when they were splendid in the green valley of youth, he felt the agony and the loss.

The writing of the novel *The Black Prophet* did, he said, involve the heartrending consideration of life and death to an extent beyond all historic precedent, not an abstract consideration of the mysteries of birth and life and death, creation and procreation and the final end of soul and body. Novelists being men and seeing and knowing and experiencing mortality have been drawn powerfully to such abstract consideration. But only a few novelists have written of death in the middle of universal death. He felt that the choice of subject necessitated the explanation of motives, a statement of intentions going above and beyond artistic election or artistic necessity. So he pointed out that, seeing in the autumn of 1846 the failure of the potato crop it had occurred to him that a story based on the famine made almost inevitable by that failure would 'awaken those who legislate for us into something like a humane perception of a calamity that has been almost perennial in the country.' It might stir inactive sympathy into active and efficient benevolence. 'National inflictions of this kind pass away, and are soon forgotten by everyone but those with whom they have left their melancholy memorials, to wit, the widow, the fatherless, the destitute, and all who look in vain around their desolate hearths for those on whose love and labour they had depended for the very means of sustaining life. Aware of this, then, and knowing besides, that the memory of our legislature is as faithless on such a subject as that of the most heartless individual among us, the author deemed it an act of public usefulness to his countrymen, to record . . . such an authentic history of those deadly periods of famine . . . as could be relied upon with confidence by all who might feel an interest in placing them beyond the reach of this terrible scourge.'

He assured his English and Scottish readers that he had not coloured the truth. He had written down what he had seen in 1817 and 1822, years of emphasised famine. In other places and at other times he was to write down what he had seen or heard of in the greater horror of Black '47. Then he dedicated the book to the Prime Minister of Great Britain and Ireland.

Over the doomed country men, bent in fear, saw signs and omens in the sky. The clouds were black like the black drapery of the grave, and in their slow movement they took to themselves the shapes of hearses and coffins and long funeral processions, scattered now and again by the lightning that followed the long roll of thunder. Under such a sky his story began, in a glen called the black glen, for the colour of the sultry clouds was after all only a reflection of the desolation on the earth and in the hearts and souls of men. 'Go where you might,' he wrote, 'every object reminded you of the fearful desolation that was progressing around you. The features of the people were gaunt, their eyes wild and hollow, and their gait feeble and tottering. Pass through the fields, and you were met by little groups bearing home on their shoulders, and that with difficulty, a coffin, or perhaps two of them. The roads were literally black with funerals; and, as you passed along from parish to parish, the death bells were pealing forth.'[1]

[1] *The Black Prophet.*

123

Skies black with ominous thunder clouds, fields black where the roots and the plants had rotted in the furrows, roads black with the weary processions of death. The terrible word repeats itself again and again like a recurring lament, the negation of colour, the negation of all life. In the black glen the black-haired daughter of the black prophet quarrels violently with the woman who is supposed to be the black prophet's wife, and all through the terrible scene that ends in a demoniacal struggle and the accidental discovery of a tobacco-box bearing the initials of a man mysteriously murdered in the days of the rebellion, the feeling of gloom and darkness accumulates. It was a melodramatic beginning for a very melodramatic story, filled with wild coincidences and misleading identities and extravagant gestures. But there is no denying the historical authenticity or the artistic effectiveness of that carefully erected background. 'How black the evenin' is gatherin',' says one of the two women when the terrible quarrel has ended like a roll of thunder passing off along the sky. And out on the road Black Donnel the prophet cries out to a neighbour in rhythmic words that give meaning and dignity to the lingo of the prophecy-man: 'Look about you, and say what it is you see that doesn't fortell famine—famine—famine! Doesn't the dark wet day, an' the rain, rain, rain, fortell it? Doesn't the rottin' crops, the unhealthy air, an' the green damp fortell it? Doesn't the sky without a sun, the heavy clouds, an' the angry fire of the West foretell it? Isn't the earth a page of prophecy, an' the sky a page of prophecy, where every man may read of famine, pestilence an' death. The earth is softened for the grave, an' in the black clouds of heaven you may see the death-hearse movin' slowly along—funeral after funeral—funeral after funeral—an' nothing to follow them but lamentation an' woe, by the widow an' orphan—the fatherless, the motherless, an' the childless—woe an' lamentation—lamentation an' woe.'

For an illustrated edition of the story, published in the last year of the nineteenth century,[1] the pencil of J. B. Yeats, the father of the poet and of a greater painter than himself, caught in a striking drawing the posture of Black Donnel telling of desolation in a desolate land. In everything else, except his love for his wild daughter, the black prophet was a calculating liar, imposing on the credulity of the people, concealing his lies in a complicated dressing of whorled and antique phrases. His hand was red with human blood. But when he stood on the wet road in the middle of a decaying harvest, chanting and gesturing his story about the greater desolation to come, he became for a moment towering and symbolic, a voice out of the black sky, a cry from the weary hungry earth insistently claiming its own. His words went out over fields where even the

[1] By Lawrence & Bullen of London. With an introduction by D. J. O'Donoghue.

few crops that were ripe had a sickly and unthriving look, where crops that in other autumns would have been ripe and yellow were thin and backward and unnaturally green, over low meadows flooded by the incessant rain, over fields where the ravages of floods were still visible in layers of mud and gravel lying heavy on the prostrate corn. In the bogs the peat lay in oozy and neglected heaps, lacking the sun to dry it for use, leaving the people at the mercy of the approaching winter, without food and without fuel. Weeds grew high in the unnatural wet heat, and hedges and woods were brooding and silent for the birds had ceased to sing, and there was heard only the sullen roar of rivers in flood or the hiss of water in the swamped grasses. Over all this and including all this was the terrible chant of Black Donnel, swelling like high water around little houses in sodden fields where the people crouched down before calamity and died.

He had written of so many happy, contented homes that his pictures of plague-stricken cabins are by contrast hellish in detailed accurate vividness. In the novel *The Red-Haired Man's Wife* the old priest, Father Moran, remembers the days of 1839 when the fever that followed famine was bad and brief, and the poor dying in hundreds in their cabins, by the roadside, in the fields, in the ditches, in the lanes. The potato crop was black with blight. There was a murrain among the cattle, a failure in several of the branch banks where thrifty farmers had placed their meagre savings, and 'above and before all the black remorseless plague, which, with a cruel besom, swept the whole country from end to end.' Father Moran and his curate and the Protestant rector worked together for the suffering and the dying, and in burying the dead, riding out through the country from house to house, finding one house where a score of famished ragged creatures clustered around the door, clapping their hands and groaning and crying like animals. Crossing the threshold the three men found the quite conventional scene of the living and the dead lying together on the same rotten straw, the living not sufficiently alive to know that the dead were dead, the air solid with the stench of excrement and fever and putrefying flesh.

He saw the homes of the Irish poor in all the varieties and stages of hopeless decline, oppressed by landlordism, rejected even by the God the people worshipped. God—they were told—had sent the blight as a visitation. The pitiless skies sent the dark weather and the endless, monotonous rain. In the farmhouse of Jerry Sullivan, in the opening chapters of *The Black Prophet,* there were, just as in the signs in the clouds, prophecies of the desolation to come. The thatch on the roof had begun to blacken and in places to sink into rotten ridges. The yard was untidy, the walls and hedges broken and dismantled, the chimneys—from which the thatch had sunk down—standing up with the incrustations of lime, that had been trowelled round their bases, projecting uselessly out from them. Walking through the heart of Ireland on his way to Dublin his quick eye had photographed such telling details; his memory kept them for ever as symbols of decline and desolation. Inside the house the floor, once smooth, would be breaking into holes; the tables and chairs would be creaking and crazy; the dresser would have a cold, hungry and unfurnished look. The chimney-brace, once heavy with sides and flitches of deep, fat bacon, grey with salt, would now have nothing but bare, dust-covered hooks, or a dozen herrings hung at one side of a worn salt-box, or a small string of onions. While the man of the house might entertain his guest to the little he had to give, the children would stand around silently watching the food 'with those yearning looks that take their character from the hungry and wolfish spirit which marks the existence of a "hard year" as it is called in our unfortunate country, and which, to a benevolent heart, forms such a sorrowful subject for contemplation.'

A hard year was—in a land in which more than two million people lived always on the verge of starvation—almost a normal year. Famine meant something much more fearful. Famine meant twenty-three human beings, of all ages and sexes, as the public officers said, lying together on the same straw-littered floor, five or six of them already putrid corpses. Those who still lived were 'so completely maddened by despair, delirium, and the rackings of intolerable pain . . . that all the impulses of nature and affection were not merely banished from the heart, but superseded by the most frightful peals of insane mirth, cruelty and the horrible appetite of the ghoul and vampire. Some were found tearing the flesh from the bodies of the carcases that were stretched beside them. Mothers tottered off under the woeful excitement of misery and frenzy, and threw their wretched children on the side of the highways, leaving them there, with shouts of mirth and satisfaction, to perish or be saved . . . whilst fathers have been known to make a wolfish meal upon the dead bodies of their own offspring.'[1]

That was famine. Those things were little more than the commonplaces of famine. Famine meant hungry crowds roaming the country, their appearance in frightful harmony with the wasted land, the unreaped crops, the plashy and fermenting ruin. Almost too weak and worn to walk, the torments of hunger drove them at times to tumult and robbery, a voiceless violence, a shouting like the shouting of ghosts for 'the wretched people were not able to shout.' During the frenzied progress of some spasmodic act of pillage men and women and boys and girls could be seen seated behind ditches, or

[1] *The Black Baronet.*

in the porches of houses or out openly on the roads and streets ravenously gobbling raw flour or oatmeal, or tearing and devouring stolen bread with the unnatural appetite of famished maniacs. Following on these frantic feasts came inevitably fits of giddiness and retchings and convulsions that ended often in tormented, twisted death. Famine meant that miserable women in the early mornings went out along the trenches and ditches gathering weeds for food, happy in the finding of a few handfuls of nettles or chicken-weed or sorrel to bring home to the children. Famine sent men secretly to stock-farms in various parts of the country to bleed rich men's cattle and to drink the hot blood. Funerals no longer caused pity or comment or interest. When the dead were buried at all they were covered hastily in shallow pits, deprived even of the last sad ceremonies that dignify death and comfort the living.

Famine meant that self-respect and modesty and an independence that had existed in spite of landlordism, all those things that the people valued in themselves and William Carleton valued in the people, went like dust on the poisonous wind. 'Under the terrible pressure of the complex destitution which prevailed, everything like shame was forgotten, and it was well known that whole families, who had hitherto been respectable and independent, were precipi-tated, almost at once, into all the common cant of importunity and clamour during this frightful struggle between life and death.'[1] Around the soup-shops, wild crowds, ragged and sickly and wasted to skin and bone, struggled and screamed like vultures around a carcase, 'and the timid girl, or modest mother of a family, or decent farmer, goaded by the same wild and tyrannical cravings, urged their claims with as much turbulent solicitation and outcry as if they had been trained since their very infancy to all the forms of impudent cant and imposture.' While the good went down like animals to such degradation, the greedy strong farmer with food stored in his barn and the profiteering meal-monger with stocks on his shelves and in the room behind the shop, knew days of evil power and evil profit. Darby Skinadre, the miser, a thin and mealy man, shuffled about his shop, wearing no coat but wearing a waistcoat to which were attached flannel sleeves, pitying his poor penniless begging customers for God's sake, but refusing meal on credit for the sake of business.

For God was high and far away and heedless in heaven, and business and the making of money were still close at hand on the withering earth. Unalterable economic law, and the wickedness, conscious and unconscious, of the human heart, and the wisdom of the nineteenth century were on the earth. Landlords living in high houses owned the earth, seized for the rent the little amount of corn

[1] *The Black Prophet.*

that might have saved the lives of the people, sent it in carts to the sea-harbours for export. Down the same roads went the staggering people, no longer believing in the good earth, fleeing from hell in the cabins, and ditches, running from the last land of Europe, from the island of traditional romantic greenery that had suddenly smelt of pestilence and turned black under the black sky. Against the spectacle of that exodus, as always against the spectacle of famine and war and the poor needlessly condemned, the story of human progress can be as pitiful as a tale told casually on a dusty weary afternoon, and the human heart can seem suddenly as foul as the earth that rotted and dragged down to corruption a whole miserable people.

It was not one year or two years or three. When there was not the deepest horror of famine there was the threat of famine. There was always hunger. There were always the two millions who could never be sure of their food. It was not confined to the island on which Carleton lived his life and wrote his books. But nowhere else in Europe were the poor so utterly neglected. In no other country could a man writing to interpret a people be faced so terribly with the task of interpreting what looked like the total extinction of that people. A writer could hardly feel that his work would go to found or strengthen a distinctive literary tradition; and when the smell of death became too strong and the only colour in the world was the denial of all colour, the creative artist could do little more than record atrocity after atrocity, writing pamphlet material that has value to-day because of the merciless character of its realism.

The opening pages of *The Squanders of Castle Squander* had bright moments of humour and tatterdemalion gesture as strong as anything in the stories of Neal Malone, the tailor, or of Phelim O'Toole. But the final pages fall in the best pamphleteering style to the quoting of statistics and reports and learned reviews. The subject was famine, and even the dullest quotation had the power of taking to itself a very morbid interest-value. But through these columns of figures and recorded facts Lady Squander went travelling one day to the graveyard in which her husband lay buried. It was a significant journey; for Lady Squander was the essence of Squanderism, the pure spirit of Irish landlordism that had ruined the people because of greed and extravagance, that was bringing landlord and tenant down to the same end in the bitter earth. For the first time in her life Lady Squander was travelling on the same road and in the same direction as the people of Ireland, and the road led down to the graveyard.

In that graveyard men were busy burying weak shells of coffins often not deeper than ten or twelve inches in the ground, and 'one horrific remnant of humanity, whose nearly black features retained the frightful and spasmodic contortions of cholera, was in the act of being thrown, coffinless and half-naked, into what was rather a shallow trench than a grave.' Gaunt starving dogs ravenously howled their hunger, waited for the coming of the moon and the moment when the graves were unguarded. In one place lay a mangled arm, in another a half-eaten head, in another a leg had been partially pulled from the earth, in a corner by the tottering wall a wolfish hound lay undisturbed making his meal off the features of a head held calmly between his paws.

The roads of all Ireland seemed to lead only to graveyards like the graveyard in which Squire Squander lay buried down deep, tolerably safe from the body-snatching dogs; or to ports where emigrant ships spread sail and carried mournful passengers out into the unknown; or to workhouses which were very literally next-door to the graveyards. He called these workhouses 'all Black Holes of Calcutta,' hopelessly overcrowded and understaffed, sick and quick, young and old, male and female lying in the same sweltering mass of cholera and dysentery. Anyway, among such a multitude, what could the few medical men do except die with those who died? The thirteenth report of the Poor Law Commissioners showed that fifty-four officers—including clerks, masters, medical officers, and six chaplains—died, out of 150 who caught one or other of the many available diseases. For back in 1832 cholera 'like an eastern monarch' had suffered no brother malady near the throne; in 1848 it had to help it famine-fever and dysentery and diarrhoea. And for the few public officers who died out of devotion to their duty there were naturally the many prepared to turn the deepest misery of others to their own profit. There were Poor Law Guardians who perpetrated or connived at villainy that meant worse and less food for the inmates of the black holes, 'artificial milk' that killed hundreds by a rather fearful form of diarrhoea. In those hell-holes cleanliness was seldom enforced, was anyway, under the overcrowded conditions of the apathetic sufferers, almost impossible; their shirts and shifts stiff with vermin, they sat around troughs and ate poor quality stirabout moistened with the chalky and extremely purgative milk.

In Connaught it was a common sight to meet the body-cadgers driving their donkey-carts loaded with naked corpses. 'Such a combination of many-shaped misery brooded upon the country as, perhaps, since the time of the great plague in London, was never witnessed.' Driving through the afflicted countryside, seeing the varieties of ignominy and suffering that had come upon his people, reading and hearing reports of greater horror from parts of the country he had never visited, his mind rested not with Le Sage and his creative laughter but with the frightening chronicle of plague written by Daniel Defoe. In Carleton's Ireland 'the fields and drains and ditches and morasses had over them, in them and upon them a number of suffering wretches, who moved from place to place— crawling languidly and with difficulty; some tottering, some creeping upon all fours like savage beasts of the field, and others hurrying with feeble speed to convey a portion of the wild and innutritious weeds they had picked up as a means of sustaining life in such of their helpless families as were unable, either from illness or hunger, to go abroad as their own providers.' Over all this was the silence of sultry skies, broken only by 'the cry, the groan, the insane howl, the still more frantic laughter, and solemn death-prayer, with some-times a curse so piercing and vehement that it bore the same relation to the gloom which overhung the country as the midnight lightning does to the black and lowering cloud from which it proceeds, serving only to reveal its horrors.'[1]

[1] *The Squanders of Castle Squander.*

FIFTEEN

WHAT HAD happened to London before the eyes of the author of *Moll Flanders* and *Robinson Crusoe* had been something similar to what had happened to many cities in the insanitary centuries. When plague came killing into the medieval streets it had frequently been possible to escape the smells and the contagion by flight into the clean country. Boccaccio, being of the intellectual breed of Le Sage, made that escape. But in nineteenth-century Ireland it was not the cities or the towns or undrained or unsanitary streets that caused the country places to blacken with corruption, that sent the people among whom Carleton had found Denis O'Shaughnessy and Jemmy McEvoy and Phelim O'Toole crawling like afflicted vermin on a monstrous dung-heap.

Some people said it was the English. It was so easy—easier because not always without reason—for Irishmen to curse at calamity and say: 'It is the English.' People said it was the Act of Union, or the Corn Laws, or the repeal of the Corn Laws, or the landlords, or overpopulation, or some fault in the people, or unalterable economic laws, or the precarious nature of the potato and the prevalence in Europe of the black blight. Some said even more simply that it was the hand of God and, with a resignation that possibly depended on how far tragedy was from the speaker's doorstep, many good people were prepared to leave it at that. Yet if you did believe in a God who was omnipotent and omnipresent it was only common sense to assume that God had something to do with the business, either for the sanctification and salvation of those who suffered, or for their more fortunate neighbours who could earn heaven by unstinted charity, or as a sign to the good to become better and to the wicked to amend their ways. 'Divine Providence,' wrote Father Mathew, 'in its inscrutable ways has again poured out upon us the vial of its wrath.'

The ways of divine providence were little more inscrutable than the ways of the owners of the festering soil of Ireland, little more inscrutable than the misgovernment and miscalculation that had made possible the period's odd mixture of famine on one island and frothy talk of progress on a neighbouring island. Father Mathew, travelling through the country from Cork to Dublin on the twenty-seventh day of July, 1846, had seen the 'doomed plant bloom in all the luxuriance of an abundant harvest.' Returning from Dublin to Cork on the third day of August he saw with sorrow one wide waste of putrefying vegetation. 'A blast more destructive than the simoon of the desert has passed over the land, and the hopes of the

131

poor potato-cultivators are totally blighted, and the food of a whole nation has perished.' He saw in many places the wretched people seated on the fences of their decaying gardens, wringing their hands, and wailing bitterly the destruction that left them foodless. Being a man who believed in God, the Capuchin friar very logically bowed his head before the punishment that came mysteriously on the poisonous blast. Being a man of great energy and of great practical charity he did all that he could do to help his suffering brothers. But, apart from the putrefying wind, there was all that accumulation of human greed and stupidity that had left ignorant, uninstructed people dependent on one vulnerable plant, existing in very unholy, hungry poverty, liable to wholesale extermination by any chance calamity. That greed and stupidity has little to do with the hand of God or the vials of divine wrath, except in so far as hell has a certain relation of contrast to heaven; and in every period of human history there have been such moments when selfishness hardened a creed or a class into something alien to the blue sky or the green grass or the light of the sun. Selfishness and stupidity were remaking and re-colouring the countryside of Carleton's and Father Mathew's Ireland.

Sir Charles Trevelyan was, for instance, one of the most able and enlightened civil servants that England at that time sent to Ireland to guide and direct the business of feeding the hungry. He wrote all about it in the *Edinburgh Review* in January of 1848, and the article was afterwards reprinted as a little book with the title *The Irish Crisis*. It is a conscientious record of work conscientiously done. It is the quiet, unpoetic, uninspiring testimony of the good civil servant. It has moments of humanity, exceptional in nineteenth-century officialdom, or in officialdom in any century. But it never quite escapes from the assumption that the famine was allowed by God, or by somebody, to give an opportunity for the development and improvement of theory and practice in civil service relief-organisations. It is childishly easy to misrepresent or at least to misinterpret the workings of such a mind, and a sentence lifted cruelly from its context can crackle like the laughter of a fool; but remembering always the energetic sincerity of his work, the comparative accuracy of his figures, the fact that it is easy to be wise a century after the event, it is still impossible to miss the underlying and unconscious fatuity of such a sentence as: 'Ireland had now a year and a half's experience of the administration of relief on a large scale and in different ways, and the objects to be aimed at and the abuses to be avoided had become generally known.' His meaning and the essential truth are as plain as daylight, but everything that he neglected to take into account is as monstrously ominous as the skies that blackened over a black land where an unfortunate people was experiencing other things than official relief.

Posterity, Trevelyan said, would trace back to the famine 'the commencement of a salutary revolution in the habits of a nation long singularly unfortunate.' Posterity would also acknowledge that 'on this, as on many other occasions, Supreme Wisdom has educed permanent good out of transient evil.' One sample of the permanent good would be that for the first time in the history of Ireland 'the poor man has become sensibly alive to the idea that the law is his friend.' Previously, as the good civil servant saw it, the landlords had had agents who collected their rents, and the landlords very naturally supported their agents. The grand jury had had agents to collect the county-cess, and those agents had enjoyed the protection of the grand jury. But now 'for the first time, the poor man has an agent to collect *his* rent. That agent is the poor-rate collector and he should be supported by the poor.'

The years that followed proved clearly enough the fantasticality of that vision of the lamb and the lion, the law and the poor man lying down together. But 'posterity' has made fools of wiser men than Sir Charles Trevelyan. The pitiable thing is to find a man, representative of many other men, letting everybody know in his own words that he is moving about in a world which he has not clearly realised. The landlord had his agent collecting his rent, and the agent lived, often dishonestly, at the landlord's expense, and the landlord passed the accumulating burden back by way of the agent to the broken-backed people. The horrible truth was that if landlords had had different ideas, if the agents had had different and more normal functions, the conscientious labour of Sir Charles Trevelyan would never have been necessary. A more horrible truth was that a poor-rate for the upkeep of workhouses or death-houses was only one more additional burden.

Trevelyan learned something from his experiences of Irish famine. Probably he learned as much as or more than any official of his time. He wrote down the conclusions he had arrived at as a result of 'this remarkable crisis in our national affairs, when the events of many years were crowded into two short seasons, and a foundation was laid for social changes of the highest importance.' No man who combines head and heart in the proportion that makes neither a ghoul nor a machine but a human being, no man who can feel for the sufferings of other men past or present, could read those words without being tortured with sickening pity for the crawling, stricken thousands left to the cretinous mercy of everything that Sir Charles Trevelyan represented.

He concluded, firstly, that 'it had been proved to demonstration that local distress cannot be relieved out of national funds without great abuses and evils.' Well and good.

He concluded that it had been established 'by the result of these extensive experiments in the science, if it may be so called, of relieving the destitute, that two things ought to be carefully separated which are often confounded.' The two things were improvement and relief. He was quite correct when he concluded that they should not be confused, but he was not very original. The Dickensian charity boy when he had mastered the alphabet decided it was by no means worth while going through so much to learn so little. In a similar way, Paddy, rotting in his cabin, without the strength to cover with clay the corpses of his wife and children, might have argued had he possessed sufficient breath, that given a decent chance for improvement he need never have been made the laboratory rabbit for experimenters in the very odd science discovered by Sir Charles Trevelyan.

He concluded also that the case of Ireland had at last been understood, that the abyss separating England and Ireland had, in fact, been fathomed for 'the attention of the two countries has been so long directed to the same subject, that a new reciprocity of interest and feeling has been established.' The two countries might have found a more auspicious way of bringing to birth that new reciprocity of interest and feeling; and anyway 'posterity' was to find out to its cost that the calamity of the famine was to add one more additional embitterment to the traditionally bitter story of England and Ireland.

Trevelyan claimed that the famine had disabused the Irish 'gentry' and the Irish 'lower orders' of their excessive dependence on government. Previously no gentleman would marry his daughter off without consulting the Castle; and in 1847 poor people in a part of the West had laid in no turf because they thought the Queen would supply them with coal. But now, said he, they understood 'that the proper business of a government, is to enable private individuals of every rank and profession in life to carry on their several occupations with freedom and safety.' Maybe the gentry of Ireland did understand all that. Sir Charles Trevelyan was there looking at them and should have known. But other observers at that time had come wearily to the conclusion that Ireland's landed gentry were incapable of understanding anything. William Carleton said that the monster that had destroyed a million and a quarter people was a three-headed monster. One head was famine. One head was the pestilence that followed famine. The third head was extermination by the landlords. As for the poor people who waited for the queen's coals to keep their hearth-fires burning it was most unlikely that they lived long enough to cogitate on abstractions about the functions of government. Shivering with cold and starving with hunger in stricken places beyond the Shannon they would never have considered themselves as private individuals of any rank or profession. They knew vaguely that in far-away Dublin there was a government that stood behind the landlords, and the landlords wanted rent even from men who had no food to eat. Dying and emigrating were the only two occupations that they could carry on with freedom and safety.

Sir Charles Trevelyan made his conclusions and passed on, his voice fading off towards posterity like the low hollow bellowing of a benevolent bull. He was the best that power and official might could offer in the nineteenth century to an abandoned people; and the moronic insufficiency of that best should set the powerful and the officially mighty in all ages carefully examining their consciences. In spite of his conclusions hunger remained in Ireland, and death by hunger and death by fever, and extermination by landlords, and rack-renting and evictions, and emigration sending the best of the people moving in a line without end to the harbours and the emigrant ships. The people were leaving Ireland because the only alternative was starvation in Ireland. England was sending Sir Charles Trevelyan to Ireland to bring relief to a people without food; and Ireland was steadily exporting food to England, and some of that food was being sent back to Ireland to help the relief work on which Sir Charles Trevelyan was busy. It was all as funny, as delightfully upside down as an Irish bull. Irish writers who would naturally be at home among Irish bulls had, anyway, the advantage of a local colour for which Hugo or Gautier might have cheerfully sold their souls. It hangs like a black curtain behind the movement of life in all the Irish writers of the nineteenth century who were in any way conscious of the threatened existence of the people. It turned what might have been among the best of Carleton's novels into a pamphlet that would be dull if it wasn't terrifying.

It left corners of black shadow in Michael Banim's blood-red story, *Crohoore of the Bill-Hook*. For Pierce Shea, in pursuit of the elusive hunch-backed Crohoore, came to the inevitable cabin, recently spoliated by the tithe-proctor, sought shelter there from a passing shower and saw: 'the large, waste den, with its sides rough as a quarry, and the black roof dripping rain and soot.' There was no furniture beyond a bundle of straw on which lay a shivering child, while two other children squatted listlessly on the damp floor, and, seated by the fireless hearth, was a man without shoes or stockings, coat or vest, covered only with tattered breeches and a soot-stained shirt, his arms folded hard, his chin sunk into his breast.

Etched stiffly and heavily, or sculptured in black stone, that father

135

and his motherless children could stand symbolically for the people that the Banims and Carleton used as material for novels. Looking at that scene it is easy to understand the preoccupation of Michael Banim's story with the red of blood, or the stifling preoccupation of so much of William Carleton with the dull black of desolation. He wrote *The Black Prophet* and *The Black Baronet* and *The Black Spectre* and a story with a Gaelic name that meant *The Black Day,* a story that, incidentally, left a deep impression on a lawyer called Isaac Butt.

The black shadow spreads out over the century and over the writers of the century. Jane Barlow who, according to T. W. Rolleston, closely resembled Carleton, and who, as far as Irish fiction was concerned, helped at the deathbed of the nineteenth century, found for her imagination and her art a small village of poor people in a western bog. The bogland around Lisconnel was lonely, but it was, in a sombre fashion, colourful. 'Heath, rushes, furze, ling, and the like have woven it thickly, their various tints merging, for the most part, into one uniform brown, with a few rusty streaks in it, as if the weather-beaten fell of some huge primaeval beast were stretched smoothly over the flat plain. Here and there, however, the monochrome will be broken: a white gleam comes from a tract where the breeze is deftly unfurling the silky bog-cotton tufts on a thousand elfin distaffs; or a rich glow, crimson and dusky purple dashed with gold, betokens the profuse mingling of furze and heather blooms; or a sunbeam, glinting across some little grassy *esker,* strikes out a strangely jewel-like flash of transparent green.'

Jane Barlow called that book of stories about Lisconnel by the name *Irish Idylls;*[1] and Ireland is one of those odd countries in which it is almost always possible to uncover something of the idyllic. But even in Jane Barlow's coloured land the bog could turn grey and stiffen with frost, the east wind could blow blighting, corrupting blackness into the seed-potatoes on which life in Lisconnel depended. Faces could lengthen and heads shake, superstitious minds draw omens from the flickering white flights of seagulls over the bog, from the gloomy croaking and flapping of passing herons, from 'the long trains of wild duck, scudding by like trails of smoke.' A man, distraught with famine-fever, could bolt himself and his children into the cabin while the woman of the house went searching for food; and when she returned her husband was too weak to answer her battering at the door. In the morning he and his children were dead in the cabin, the mother dead outside on the ground, and in Lisconnel they said her tormented spirit battered night after night on the closed and bolted door.

1 London, Hodder & Stoughton, 1892.

There were dark, sunless corners in the most idyllic places; and the soul of Ireland in the darkness was for all the world like the figure of the farmer standing among his rotting ridges, weighed down with all the weariness of years of poverty and oppression and hopeless hunger that had made him 'a haggard and tatterdemalion Despair.'

SIXTEEN

EXTERMINATION by the landlords, he said, was one head of the three-headed dragon devouring the people; and as he wrote he could see Deaker's Dashers riding down on the village of Drum Dhu, to do the will of Valentine McClutchy. In front rode a little, squat figure, 'all belly, with a short pair of legs at one end, and a little, red fiery face, that looked as if it would explode, at the other.' At the end of the procession came Valentine and his son Phil, and Solomon the lawyer and Darby the Bailiff, full to the neck with his own ominous importance, carrying in his hand something that looked like a baton of office but was really the roll of paper with the list of the names of those to be expelled. The doomed people gathered angrily in crowds and watched the work of eviction: battering in of doors, tearing down of the thatch, the levelling of mud-walls with the parent earth. There were women in tatters, without shoes and without stockings, carrying half-starved children in their arms. There were labouring careworn men, heads bound up in cotton handkerchiefs that indicated illness or partial recovery from illness. There were old men bent over their staves, long white hair streaming on the cold wind, their faces rigid with anger and haggard with terror.

The homes of Drum Dhu were broken, the people of Drum Dhu turned out to the roads and the ditches on a Christmas Day. Most of the facts he took from an actual eviction incident, made them coherent, fitted them into the tale of Valentine McClutchy, where they provide as good a picture of what went on at an eviction as can be found anywhere in either the creative literature or the documentation of the Irish nineteenth century. The Irish writer was never at a loss for such incidents. Protected by law, by the police, by soldiers in uniform, by Orange yeomen, the Irish landlords or their agents went out not merely to collect rents or even to collect unjust rents, but to clear away the superfluous people and free the land for profitable cattle. People no longer had any value. Once, their value had been in votes, but the political reform that with one hand had given political freedom to Catholics had with the other hand curtailed that freedom by disfranchising the forty-shilling freeholers. Lacking a vote the Irish small farmer was less, infinitely less, than the grazing cattle.

In one year and within the boundaries of one Poor Law Union 6,000 families were evicted; on one estate one hundred and twenty homes were flattened to the ground in one day. Driven from their hovels the dispossessed people were forbidden to seek shelter among the ruins; they had the ditch or the poorhouse, and there is on record a case of five evicted families living all together in one little room twelve feet square. There are other equally interesting cases; a woman sick with dysentery lying in a cowshed, and the inspector that recorded her story waded, ankle-deep in mud, to the place where she lay; a widow and three children lived for three weeks in a piggery measuring five feet by four; a temporary hut built by an evicted tenant was burned by the landlord's men while the tenant and his family were on the sea-shore close at hand gathering shell-fish for food. And so on and so on. Figures mean nothing. Details are only tiresome. The landlords were, after all, men not monsters; and if the sentimental and soft of heart should feel the cold sickness of horror when contemplating the demoniacal efforts to rid the earth of people as if people were no better than weeds, then it is wise to remember that the landlords were only obeying the economic inevitabilities of the time. That time had too its soft-hearted sentimentalists. They made their way into Westminster, and after argument an Act was passed. The Act said that when the landlord wanted to throw some-body out on the road—a bed-ridden grandfather, or a pregnant mother, or a farmer broken with poverty and slavery and fever— then the landlord might at least have the gentlemanliness to tell the local relieving officer, forty-eight hours in advance, of the meditated creation of some additional paupers. The Act also said that no eviction could take place between sunset and sunrise; and, remembering the birth and death of Christ, the Act said that nobody should be evicted on Good Friday or on Christmas Day. For of many ages in the story of man it is true to say that their abominations are most clearly revealed by their crippled attempts to grasp at goodness. It is emphatically true of Ireland in those middle years of the nineteenth century.

The abomination of injustice was leaving its mark on the country-side, joining its withering, blasting power to the desolation left by famine and fever and black blight. Evory Easel, in the course of his honest investigation into life on the Castle Cumber estate, passed by and meditated on the ruins of the deserted village of Drum Dhu. Any honest man could have seen similar sights and made similar meditations in almost any part of Ireland: 'On the roadside there were the humble traces of two or three cabins, whose little hearths had been extinguished, and whose walls were levelled to the earth. The black fungus, the burdock, the nettle, and all those offensive weeds that follow in the train of oppression and ruin were here; and as the dreary wind stirred them into sluggish motion, and piped its melancholy wail through these desolate little mounds, I could not help asking myself, if those who do these things ever think that there is a reckoning in after life, where power, and insolence and wealth misapplied, and rancour, and pride, and rapacity, and persecution, and revenge, and sensuality, and gluttony, will be placed face to face with those humble beings, on whose rights and privileges of simple existence they have trampled with such a selfish and exterminating tread.'

Figures meant nothing. Figures piled up and accumulated in long pages of long confusing columns shutting off the vision from the rapidly emptying countryside. In 1847, the blackest year of black famine, there had been 768,000 farms. Three years later 140,000 of these had been annihilated by extermination and consolidation and emigration. In 1841 there had been 310,000 farms between one and five acres; by 1850, 218,000 of these had been eliminated, not by emigration, for the men who farmed these very uneconomic holdings were too poor to emigrate; they could go only to the poorhouse or the grave. Across the sea to Liverpool, from Liverpool across the Atlantic to the New World the more fortunate sailed, frequently bringing fever with them, providing an unwelcomed problem for English local authorities. In 1847 about 300,000 of them arrived in Liverpool; only 123,000 sailed off again across the Atlantic.

But figures, even when they cannot be turned or twisted or differently interpreted to prove twenty different things, are not flesh and blood, or a land left desolate and abandoned under a lonely sky; nor can they tell any fraction of the story of human misery. Nowhere more than in *The Emigrants of Ahadarra* did he write down his own strong love for familiar country-places, detailing and lyricising until the sensitive reader can smell and see and feel the Irish countryside, happy under sun and rain, freed from the desolation that crushed it in his days, essentially unchanged and unchangeable. The spring came to it, in the first page of that book, like beauty to a growing girl. 'The month was May,' he wrote, exulting like a medieval poet rejoicing to run the race that almost always began with showers soft, and lambs frisking on green meadows inevitably enamelled with daisies. 'Nothing could be more delightful and exhilarating than the breeze which played over the green fields that were now radiant with the light which was flooded down upon them from the cloudless sun. Around, in every field, were the tokens of that pleasant labour from which the hopes of ample and abundant harvests always spring. Here, fixed in the ground, stood the spades of a *boon* of labourers, who, as was evident from that circumstance, were then at breakfast; in another place might be seen the plough and a portion of the tackle lying beside it, being expressive of the same fact. Around, on every side, in hedges, ditches, green fields, and meadows, the birds seemed animated into joyous activity or incessant battle, by the business of nest-building or love. Whilst all around, from earth and air, streamed the ceaseless voice of universal melody and song.' Years later, when he read the last paragraph of a letter written to him by his friend, Wakeman the antiquary, who was then teacher of drawing in Portora Royal School at Enniskillen, he knew how the melody and song had died into the distance, how the cheerful sound of men working in the fields had passed off into emptiness. 'This part of the country,' wrote Wakeman, 'must be greatly changed from what you will recollect of it. *All* the young people appear to have emigrated. The land is almost entirely under grass. Yesterday I had a glorious walk from this town through Derrygonnelly to Knockmore, and home by the shore of Lough Erne. In that march of about twenty-two miles I did not see more than eight people.'

With a good reaping-hook, a second-hand spade, a little whole-some food, three-and-sixpence in money, a night's lodging in Dublin, a ticket to Liverpool, Paddy was prepared for the first stage of the flight from his own accursed land: from the earth that had blackly betrayed the children of earth, from the mother that had cruelly withheld nourishment from her hungry children. He brought with him his high capacity for joy, his intense feeling for sorrow, his living coloured memories of all the things that the poet of a new Ireland was to sing about on the eve of a new century: vanished faces, cabins now fallen in ruin, old well-sides, the old dear places. Tossing over the great Atlantic he joined in all the jokes and the singing and the laughter, then sought 'a silent corner or a silent hour to indulge the sorrow which he still feels for the friends, the companions, and the native fields that he has left behind him.'[1] From the other side of the ocean the exiles wrote letters, the American letters that found their place in proverb and in popular song, en-closing the money of the great new world to help old people to live at home or young people to follow also the emigrants' way, telling of the strange places in which they found themselves, remembering the old loved places in which they had found it impossible to live, remembering the old land 'where the green shamrock, the blessed sign of the sacred and undivided Trinity grows upon our graves to keep them holy.'[2]

The exiles had their own stories and songs, to a certain extent their own civilisation. They fitted into the chaotic growing life of the extraordinary thing that was to become the greatest nation of the modern world. They rubbed shoulders and exchanged experi-ences with men of all nations in the vast spaces where the weary wounds of Europe were seeking refreshment and healing. They were

[1] 'The Party Fight and Funeral' (*Traits and Stories*).
[2] 'Barney Branagan.'

141

now a good influence and now a bad influence. They moved into lonely places in Canada and Australia and, to a lesser extent, in New Zealand. The Irish emigrant became a pathetically poetic figure, looking back over the sea to the fair hills of fair Ireland, remembering home with the rending nostalgia with which one very typical Irishman remembered his boyhood in a lost valley where he had seen in the sunshine the Ireland that almost perished, but that—in that valley and in a hundred other places—was to hold tenaciously to an imperishable life.

America, said Finigan, the drunken schoolmaster, was the *refugium peccatorum,* the overgrown cupping-glass that was drawing out of Ireland the best blood of Ireland. But the Irish, answered Bryan McMahon of Ahadarra, were lucky to have such a country to fly to, to receive them when they were neglected and overlooked in their own land. The words of Bryan and his sister Dora and their old father still open up a window into the soul of the Irish emigrant: Paddy with his bundle, with a heart now light with hope and now heavy with remembering, footing it along a hundred roads from cabins to quaysides, proverbial Paddy perpetually off to Philadelphia in the morning. By a contradiction made necessary by certain conventions of the nineteenth-century novel, the emigrants of Ahadarra never got beyond the point of making up their minds to emigrate; their world had, for the purposes of a happy ending, to turn bright again; Bryan McMahon was reconciled to and married the chaste and high-principled Cathleen Cavanagh, the villain was banged and banished, and the landlord behaved like a gentleman and renewed the leases. But all around Ahadarra were the townlands whose people could not be saved by the twist of a story or the act of a story-teller. Their townlands were cursed with poverty and famine and disease and the tyranny of the landlord, and there was no remedy but the remedy of flight into an exile where every dream, waking and sleeping, would be poignant with memories of the old places and the abandoned homesteads. 'Do you think,' said Dora McMahon, 'I'd not miss the summer sun rising behind the Althadawan hills? An' how could I live without seeing him set behind Mallybeney?'

For the young who had more hope than memories the strain of breaking and ending and beginning was bearable; their fathers and mothers needed some other impulse stronger than the desire for change or the curiosity about new lands and peoples, or mere discontentment with poverty and meagre living. Hot anger against his own countrymen drove Tom McMahon to the decision to go into exile with his children: anger with a country hopelessly divided against itself, with 'a crew of vagabonds that would sell Christ himself, let alone their country, or their religion, if they were bribed by Protestant gold for it.' His anger went out witheringly to include the worthless landlord who could in the end cheat tenants who had been faithfully honest and industrious for years, to include also the system that could allow men to be so worthless. 'For many a long year,' he told the landlord's agent, 'have our names been—but no matter—the time has come at last, and the McMahons of Carriglass and Ahadarra will be known there no more. It wasn't our fault; we were willing to live.'

But when the years had made a man too old for hope and too old for anger, there was left nothing but red memories that were almost dreams, terrible dreams holding the soul of the exile in his home when his body was torn apart and swept over the sea. The father of Tom McMahon and the grandfather of Dora looked forward only to death that would bring his white head to the clay in the graveyard of Carndhu. 'Carndhu's a holy churchyard. Sure there never was a Protestant buried in it but one, an' the next morning there was a boortree bush growin' our of the grave, an' it's there yet to prove the miracle.' Very obviously all America could offer nothing like the graveyard in Carndhu, nothing like his old home in Carriglass. For in Carriglass he had been young and active, his hair had been fair and curling like gold. In Carriglass, between the dark hills and the green fields, he had felt the years gather around him, and had found the love of Peggy Slevin, famed for her beauty and her sweet voice. 'There on the side of the hill is the roofless house where she was born; an' there's not a field or hill about the place that her feet didn't make holy to me. I remember her well. I see her, an' I think I hear her voice on the top of Lisbane, ringing sweetly across the valley of the Mountain Water.'

The words were a three-fold lamentation: for the lost boyhood of William Carleton, for the passing away of the people, for the desolation of the land that the people were leaving. In large bold letters he wrote down not the epitaph of poor young Robert Emmett, but the epitaph of the Irish people: 'We were willing to live.' Willing to live at home, to be poor at home, attached as insanely as simple people always are attached to the things of home. But a dozen irresistible forces were working powerfully to root them up and tear them painfully out of the earth. Once again it was very hard for a man to watch this exodus and not lose hope for the vanishing people and the abandoned countryside, particularly when that exodus split up his own family, sending daughters to Canada and a son to Australia. The best of the people were leaving their homes, because for obvious reasons only the farmer of some little substance could afford to emigrate. The utterly poverty-stricken could afford only beggary or death. But, when the twist of the story kept the McMahons still in possession of Carriglass and Ahadarra, their creator may really have been doing something more important than following the convention of the nineteenth-century novel that violated all laws human and divine in making Wilkins Micawber a success in Australia. He may have been following the instinct of the ancient story-tellers who sent so many heroes happily through the country of the gods to restore happiness to their own homes. He may, also, have been writing a message of hope for his own people who would not die in spite of universal death, who could lose thousands of sons and daughters to help in the building of new nations, who could still survive with a fierce resilience to take possession at last of the fields in which they had known hunger, and in those green places to dig the foundations for a new nation.

SEVENTEEN

HE IS AMONG the greatest, possible the greatest writer of fiction that Ireland has given to the English language. He wrote good stories and he wrote very inferior stories; he wrote well and he wrote at times with an excruciating badness; he wrote always with a certain spontaneous outpouring of things seen and heard and vividly remembered, with little evidence that he had ever given more than a moment of his mind to models or forms or the practices of other writers. He would have gladly thought that he had done for Ireland what Walter Scott had done for Scotland, allowed himself to be flattered by the facial resemblance that in his early days he bore to the estimable author of *Waverley,* was possibly quite complimented when Daniel O'Connell referred to him as the Walter Scott of Ireland. But the wide humanity of Scott that could raise common beggars to the high dignity of kings had nevertheless to approach the beggar from the outside, at times with a fatal altruism, at times with a fatal antiquarianism. Carleton was in his high moments neither altruist nor antiquary; he was himself one of the beggars, speaking and moving and laughing and weeping with an intimacy that began in the soul. His great admiration for Scott dragged him at times away from that inner place where he was strong, to creaking efforts to emulate that great power of bringing the past back, giving movement and voices to the mighty dead. If Walter Scott had made Rob Roy MacGregor the hero of a great story there was nothing in the wide world to prevent William Carleton making a hero of Redmond Count O'Hanlon, the rapparee who had in his time in the mountains of Southern Ulster taken to himself the titles of Protector of the rights and properties of his benefactors and contributors, and chief Ranger of the mountains, surveyor-general of all the high roads of Ireland, or lord-examiner of all passengers. Wordsworth, out of his abysmal respectability, had written a 'noble ballad' with a first verse saying that Robin Hood was a famous man and the English ballad-singer's joy, but that Scotland had a thief as good and boasted her brave Rob Roy. Augustin Thierry in his *Norman Conquest* had 'taken great pains to show us the significance of the careers of the men whom Robin Hood, whether he be a real or imaginary outlaw, typifies.'

Ireland was as rich in rapparees and robbers as in persons of the Romish religion. Redmond Count O'Hanlon, the greatest of all Irish rapparees, had ridden and robbed and lived gallantly in the mountains to the East of Carleton's country. In his youth Carleton had read 'with more avidity than its literary merits warranted, a curious little chap-book, written by one J. Cosgrave, and sold no doubt extensively to the Irish peasantry at fairs and markets.' It was called: 'The Lives and Actions of the Most Notorious Irish Highwaymen, Tories, and Rapparees; from Redmond O'Hanlon to Cahier na Gappul; To which is added the Goldfinder or the History of Manus Maconiel.' With this antiquarian detail at his hand, with a dozen folk-tales in his head, with the full authority of Thierry, Wordsworth and Walter Scott, he still failed miserably to draw back out of the mists the great figure of Galloping O'Hanlon.[1] Admiration for Scott could make him attempt at least twice to echo the Jeanie Deans theme, once in the story of Ellen Duncan and once in one of his early tales; could make him write enthusiastically: 'The hand of the mighty wizard has given to immortality an humble woman for refusing to swear a lie—for performing a journey to London in order to save a sister's life.' But the mightiest wizardry of the mighty wizard necessitated a reverence for the past, even a devotion to the oddities of the past, neither of which William Carleton ever possessed. In an unpublished sketch[2] he satirised antiquarianism and made the antiquarian say: 'I thought I did not properly belong to the present time, wherein I felt myself as if by accident only, and the impression was strong upon me that I was nothing more or less than a living antique.'

Not only by choice but by the limitations of education and imagination William Carleton belonged to his own time with a completeness that swept him along in the current of contemporary life, identifying his work with the bright days and equally with the black skies of the world in which he lived, identifying his own character in a remarkably intimate way with the characters to whom he gave new and lasting life. The people who tragically kept calling him an Irish Burns writing in prose were awkwardly expressing at least a part of the truth. For Burns was and is not only a popular poet but a legendary figure in the part of Ireland from which William Carleton came. The echoes of the ploughman's songs and poems came across the sea to the ears of the young Irishman growing up into a closer contact with literary things. Like Burns he had learned a great deal from poor men and women, and a little, very little, from the pages of books. Carlyle writing of Burns could, with little alteration, have been writing of Carleton: 'What warm, all-comprehending fellow-feeling; what trustful, boundless love; what generous exaggeration of the object loved! His rustic friend, his nut-brown maiden, are no longer mean and homely, but a hero

---

[1] Francis Carlin, an Irish poet who died in the U.S.A., wrote his great *Ballad of Douglas Bridge* in praise of O'Hanlon's men; and Philip Rooney has written around O'Hanlon a fine story: *North Road.*

[2] O'Donoghue, vol. ii.

and a queen whom he prizes as the paragons of Earth. The rough scenes of Scottish life, not seen by him in any Arcadian illusion, but in the rude contradiction, in the smoke and soil of a too harsh reality, are still lovely to him: Poverty is indeed his companion, but Love also, and Courage, the simple feelings, the worth, the nobleness, that dwell under the straw roof, are dear and venerable to his heart: and thus over the lowest provinces of man's existence he pours the glory of his own soul; and they rise, in shadow and sunshine, softened and brightened into a beauty which other eyes discern not in the highest.'

A lot from men and women; a little, very little, from books; a little also from the contacts that life brought him with men of his own time who were also busy in the writing of books. Writing with his sight failing and old age creeping on he told a friend that the autobiography would certainly be an important work for in it he meant to include a general history of Irish literature, 'its origin, its progress, its decline, and its natural and progressive extension.' Ireland could point with pride, he said, only to three names: the name of Gerald Griffin, the name of John Banim, and, 'do not accuse me of vanity,' the name of William Carleton. No one could with justice accuse him of unreasoning vanity; but the sweeping nature of that statement might raise doubts as to whether he had the balance or the equipment necessary for a survey of the origin, development, decline and revival of Irish literature. Anyway death cut across the splendid plans for an important work, left the autobiography not a history of literature, but, much more appropriately, a testimony to the days of boyhood and youth, when he had grown up so close to the people that in his old age he was able to write with a touch of prophecy of days to come: 'Banim and Griffin are gone, and I will soon follow them—*ultimus Romanorum*, and after that will come a lull, an obscurity of perhaps half a century, when a new condition of civil society and a new phase of manners and habits among the people—for this is a *transition* state—may introduce new fields and new tastes for other writers.'

When the new revival came, not half a century but about thirty years later, it came as the prelude not only to transition but to transition in revolution. Its great writers were working harder than ever in the quarry that William Carleton had opened, rediscovering also the merits of Carleton. For the songs and stories he had heard from his parents and the language in which he had heard them became a strange, rejuvenating force to Irishmen writing in English; an explosive, inspirational force to Irishmen experimenting in politics. The tattered people that he had seen in glory and in agony were winning the hearts of young women and young poets from the big

147

families, and the greatest of all Irish poets was trying his hardest to tell the world that his country was Kiltartan Cross and his countrymen Kiltartan's poor. With Lever in Florence, gathering material for his stories in a life of perpetual banqueting that cost him about £1,200 a year, that new ruthlessly-Irish Ireland could have had little notable sympathy. Lever, defending himself against charges of extravagance, pointed out that his expenditure was not a luxury but a necessity, that it fed his lamp which otherwise would have died into darkness, that his banquets and receptions were really his opportunities for studying characters and picking up a thousand invaluable details. 'You can't keep drawing wine off the cask perpetually, and putting nothing in; and this is my way of replenishing it.' But, looking back at Lever, the new Ireland would naturally prefer him filling his cask with yellow whisky or black porter, than with the red and white wines of continental places, would prefer him when he wrote that to the shrewd observer of human nature the book of the human heart was nowhere opened as in Ireland. 'Where do passions, feelings, prejudices, lie so much on the surface? And where is the mystery that wraps the anomalous condition of human nature more worthy of study? Where, amid poverty and hardship, are such happiness and contentment to be met—natural and ever ready courtesy—the kind and polite attention, the free hospitality, as in the Irish peasant? Where is self most forgotten in all this wide and weary world? We answer fearlessly, in the cabin of the poor Irishman. We have travelled in most countries of the old continent, and much of the new, and we know of nothing either for qualities of heart or head, to call their equal.'[1]

Not at all averse to thinking that it possessed almost everything a little better than everybody else, the new Ireland could return with pleasure to that line of talk. It could remember, too, in Carleton's favour that, in spite of the large number of people that at one time or another he had rubbed the wrong way, he had known the inside of the Irishman's cabin and the inside of his heart in a way always impossible to Lever, impossible even to John Banim or Michael Banim or Gerald Griffin. He had taken social customs, some peculiar to Ireland of his time, more of them existing practically unchanged in the opening years of a new century, and written great stories around them. He had seen the tragedy of famine, the beginning of mass-emigration, and had written great novels, with black backgrounds of hunger and perpetually moving backgrounds of exodus and abandonment. He had looked back at a highwayman who was a national hero and gathered together in a little book some of the daring galloping stories of the great O'Hanlon. He had heard a popular ballad that was almost a national institution and written around

[1] *Dublin University Magazine*, vol. xiv, p. 98.

it the most popular of all his novels, telling the story of Willy Reilly and Helen Folliard and her father, the squire, and beauty and adventure, and elopement and banishment, and true love in the end triumphant. In a dozen places he had analysed, not without wisdom, the ills of the Ireland of his time, and had suggested remedies for those ills.

In spite of the contradictions in his own soul, in spite of the terror of his time, he was the greatest laugher his country produced, until James Joyce, seeking in exile a refuge from contradiction, looking back at one great Dublin day that comprehended all time and hinted at eternity, heard the randy laughter of the streets and the pubs, saw the dark figure and the divided soul of Stephen Dedalus. With Carleton as with Joyce Ireland joined in the laughter, knowing it genuinely for the native laughter, but always resenting the recording of hollow unhumorous echoes that every Irishman had been trying hard to forget. Phil Purcell's pigs, tall and loose and with unusually long legs, no flesh, short ears as if they had been cropped for sedition, long faces of a highly intellectual cast, an activity that surpassed greyhounds and beagles, were undeniably funny. But Irish readers following their uproariously devastating career on English farms could feel uneasily that the character of Phil and the waywardness of his pigs revealed to the world something about Ireland that was not in the least humorous, something unkempt and lawless and uncouth. Phelim O'Toole was Carleton's most laughable creation; but when Phelim's fond mother, looking at her son with the eyes of love, said: 'Doesn't he become the pock-marks well, the crathur?' and his father, looking at Phelim with the eyes of pride and hope for the half-acre, said, 'Doesn't the droop in his eye set him off all to pieces?' they had innocently hinted at an abyss of pain and pathetic deformity that made all laughter as thin as froth from broken water. To be able to convey in that way the delicate fragility of human joy, always transient, frequently depending for its existence on the human power for unconscious self-deception, may be just one of the faculties of a comprehensive, creative spirit. But in Carleton's Ireland it made pitifully obvious the fact that all joy was only a little, brief light against wide, overshadowing gloom, that all dancing was over the grave or under the gallows. Never forgetful of the method of the old story-teller he pulled his chair to the corner of the fire, told his listeners tales that were humorous or sad or terrible. But he never equalled the story-teller by the hearth in the ability to make his listeners forget that outside the closed door there was rain and the buffeting wind and the black night.

EIGHTEEN

MOORE died in 1852, fading quietly out of life like the last liquid linked sweetness of one of the melodies that interpreted his own rose-coloured Ireland, his own rose-coloured world. John Hogan, the poverty-stricken sculptor whose genius preserved for ever several of the great figures of that time, had once submitted a model for the design of a Moore statue; and when, with Hogan in the grave, Carleton was appealing for help for the sculptor's widow and orphans, he wrote in the *Irish Quarterly Review* a tribute not only to Hogan but to the poet. 'I have had the honour and pleasure,' he wrote, 'of knowing the great poet personally—well and closely did I study his features. I have heard him sing his own songs accompanied by himself on the piano; and at the conclusion of each song there was uniformly an upturning of the eyes, which flashed and sparkled with such a radiance of inspiration as I never witnessed before nor ever expect to witness again. Whether John Hogan ever saw Thomas Moore or not I cannot say—but this I can say, that the model which he conceived and executed for his monument would have given Moore to the world in the very fervour of inspiration with which he usually concluded his own songs.' As it happened Hogan's model was not accepted, and at the corner of College Street in the City of Dublin a statue was erected, to be abused by Carleton as 'one of the vilest jobs that ever disgraced the country, such a stupid abomination as has made the whole kingdom blush with indignation and shame.' The unfortunate statue, carved comically enough by a man called Moore, became later, because of the proximity of a public lavatory, the subject of popular jokes on the dead poet who had sung of friendship and sweet Avoca and the meeting of the waters. The popular jokes swept upwards from Dublin groundcurrents to touch the surface again in the meditations of Leopold Bloom; and changed times were causing men to think that Tom Moore had exactly the site and the statue he deserved. But across the best part of a century it is refreshing and illuminating to consider the days when the poet and the sculptor and the story-teller came into association and knew each other for remarkable men.

Moore brought with him to the grave, or left after him in some of his poems, the ineffectual ardour of the time when Robert Emmett had plotted and dreamed and cried out that no man should write his epitaph until Ireland was a nation. The men of Young Ireland, remembering Tone and Emmett and in their turn to influence young men in the future, had been broken and scattered by the law to the new, distant lands in which a large proportion of the Irish people were seeking refuge from poverty and hunger. Irish politics had drifted into the doldrums; and when a modern Irishman looks around for a convenient historic precedent for political corruption, he thinks of Sadleir and Keogh and the 'Pope's Brass Band', and the decadent characters of that time. In 1855 Charles Gavan Duffy who sat in parliament for New Ross wrote a retiring address to his constituents, and by implication to the people of Ireland, and sailed round the world to make a great success of himself far away in Australia. He had determined to retire 'from all share and responsibility in the public affairs of Ireland' until better times returned; and, while a captious person might have justifiably argued that the way to bring about the return of better times was not by retiring to Australia, he did undeniably give solid reasons for refusing any longer to expend energy and breath as a member of the Irish Parliamentary Party.

He pointed out that the Irish popular party was reduced to an ineffective handful, deserted even by those who had created it, opposed by many members of the Catholic hierarchy. In public life shameless profligacy was openly defended and applauded; and the party that had commenced its life with fifty members had lost forty of the fifty to the ranks of its opponents, and in general there was 'no more hope for the Irish cause than for the corpse on the dissecting-table.' The Catholic Archbishop of Dublin 'who was foremost and loudest to pronounce for the principle of independent opposition, lends all the weight of his authority to its opponents.' The majority of the Irish bishops had followed his example and the few popular patriots left uncorrupted had been 'disparaged from popular hustings, and in pastoral letters, for no sin that I know of but because we will not sell ourselves to the enemies of our country.' The public action of the priesthood had been deliberately fettered and 'the boldest of the patriot priests had been banished from public life, and remain banished.' Sadleir and Keogh had made their own party within the party, winning popularity for themselves by violent opposition to the Ecclesiastical Titles Bill and by such noisy defence of all causes Catholic that they earned from the public that ironic title of Pope's Brass Band. Irish political life no longer offered any hope to an honest man. 'Quitting public life,' wrote Duffy, 'I will quit, at the same time, my native country. I cannot look on in dumb inaction at her ruin. I cannot sit down under the system of corruption and terrorism established among us.'

Corruption and terrorism in political life. A people bled white by famine and emigration. The good and great, dead or banished or going out to give themselves to the making of young nations because their own, ancient, broken nation would not have them. The corpse on the dissecting table. Dumb inaction. Griffin and Banim

151

dead and William Carleton left—*ultimus Romanorum.* It was a poor land for a man in the end of his day. It was a poor land for ending old things or beginning new things. William Carleton knew that; growing old and gathering around him dreams and memories. John Henry Newman was to make that discovery, reading out in a hall to a Dublin audience the 'cloistral, silver-veined' sentences that made up the lectures on university education. Caught awkwardly between the wishes of the hierarchy and the talents of revolutionary young men that he would gladly have had lecturing in his new university, Newman was to wish with all his heart that he had never seen Ireland. But Newman could recross the sea to England, could console himself anyway with his sense of high spiritual mission, with the feeling that 'all who take part with the Apostle are on the winning side.'

William Carleton thought of following into exile the two beloved daughters who had gone across the sea to Canada. But all around the world from Australia came a letter from Gavan Duffy, the great cry of heart speaking to heart across unknown lands and illimitable oceans, the cry of Ireland in exile calling to Ireland, the testimony of one man for another that stands as high as a mountain above all the carping and criticism of lesser men. 'Do not dream of Canada, my friend; an oak of the forest will not bear transplanting. Even a shrub like myself does not take kindly all at once to the new climate and soil. I never for a moment regretted having left Ireland where Judge Keogh and Archbishop Cullen predominate; but the slopes of Howth, the hills of Wicklow, and the friends of manhood are things not to be matched in this golden land.' Far away in Australia the Irish emigrant was making himself at home, preserving the rural life that his counterpart had willingly abandoned when he walked across the boundaries of the great American cities. Duffy told Carleton that he would enjoy most of all in Australia the reincarnation of the Irish farmhouse 'with all the rude plenty of thirty years ago revived' as Carleton and Duffy remembered it in Monaghan and Tyrone. 'But it would need the author of the *Traits and Stories* to describe the strange hybrid, an Australian-Irish farmer with the keenness and vigour of a new country infused into his body. I am just returned from my election, where they fought for me like lions in the name of the poor old country; and to do them justice, Protestants as well as Catholics. We have bigots here, but the love of country is a stronger passion than bigotry in the heart of the exile.' [1]

At home or abroad that love of country could be an emptiness in the heart, an unforgettable torment in the bones. And why, in God's name, should men remember with such torturing sentiment a land that had given them nothing but hunger? Walking by the round

[1] O'Donoghue, vol. ii.

waters of Dublin Bay, as lonely as Ossian the poet after the passing of the Fenians, William Carleton was at liberty to speculate on that mystery. North of him, and lying in dark blue laziness across the light blue water was the hill of Howth. South of him and sharp against the sky were the two conical mountains across the county-border in Wicklow, differing in colour and character from the round Dublin hills circling lazily above the city. Duffy in Australia could close his eyes and see those hills and long for them with the passion of the exile. Carleton in Dublin could see them dimly through ageing eyes, could remember Duffy, and dream of his daughters in Canada, and dream of men and women and places that had been, and because of him would be for ever.

He could dream of his father's stories and his mother's songs, knowing with satisfaction in his own age that he had taken up the business of story-telling where his father had left off, had spoken in a different language to a different, wider world. In naming the novel *The Red-Haired Man's Wife,* that was not published until after his death, he was remembering his mother's sweetest song, the song she sang with reluctance in an English translation because the new words quarrelled with the old music. But strangely enough the shapeless, wandering novel that he wrote under that name had no word in it of the song as Blind Raftery, the Connaught poet, had written it, as James Stephens, poet and friend of the fairies, was to hear it in the opening years of a new century when he, with others, was eagerly listening to and drawing inspiration from voices speaking out of buried decades. Douglas Hyde, whom James Stephens called the fairy godfather of the new Ireland, followed in the counties across the Shannon the footsteps of Antony Raftery, gathered together all his Gaelic songs with their faint echoes of the classical Gaelic tradition and their tattered scraps from Greece and Rome hanging crazily around a body of pure poetry. He collected also the stories behind the songs: the story of Mary Hynes whose beauty broke men's hearts and in the end broke her own; and the beauty of the song the blind poet made of Mary Hynes has haunted Irish poets for fifty years.[1] The story of the tailor who jettisoned the grace of God and trampled on the laws of men for the sake of the red-haired man's wife had all the elements of high romance. Carleton must have heard it, or heard some altered version of it; for the song itself passing from lip to lip had one version in Connaught and another in Ulster. But the novel for which he borrowed the name of the song swung pitifully between the promising adventures of a lout who strolled from market to market jilting all the girls of the country, and the

[1] Yeats and Stephens tried to echo it in English. Padraic Fallon has succeeded where they failed.

153

Victorian approaches of his brother to the heart of a young lady who bore as much resemblance to the red-haired man's wife as an aged nun to Cleopatra. The young fellow even took it upon him to assist the young lady and her sister to an improved knowledge of the civilised language of the French nation. For their benefit he read and translated the novels of Erckmann-Chatrian—'which just then were beginning to attract considerable notice from the reading public on account of the very interesting record which they gave of peasant life in Alsace and the vivid pictures of scenery in that and other departments not generally visited by travellers.'

All that was very nice, but it indicated terribly two pitiful things: not only was Carleton's creative power gone, but he was trying so hard to be educated that when—almost certainly—a great story, raw and bleeding with life, was under his hand, he turned from it to write of the polite life in which he was never naturally at home. That tendency was never quite absent from his work, except in its highest moments. It is in most of those hideous early tales that he wrote for Caesar Otway, in the abomination of 'Father Butler', in 'The Brothers'. It is as unpleasantly unreal as a defensive complex always is, for the young man from the cabins whose way of life had changed when he walked up to Dublin and became a writer, was defending himself in the worst possible way against the superiority of people born in high houses. At moments that complex evidenced itself in an effort to interpret ways of life about which he knew little or nothing. Almost every novelist has at some time or other made that mistake. But when he tried to interpret his own people and at the same time to be superior to his own people, when he tried to see them as a gentleman on horseback going the road past a boon of labouring men would see them, he was making a mistake more serious than the mistake of a novelist trying to do something outside his ability.

For some reason peculiar to the period in which it was written *Jane Sinclair* was a very popular novel. The alternative title was *The Fawn of Springvale,* and Jane was the fawn, and the fawn fell in love, was elegantly deserted, went pathetically mad, and died in a decline. The opening description of Springvale was idyllic, possibly too idyllic for hungry Ireland, certainly too idyllic to act as a background for the villainy of the black prophet or the flirtations of Phelim O'Toole. So when Carleton peopled that lovely valley he introduced characters that possibly never had their like on sea or land. The first incident of the story sent Jane's pet dove floating wounded on the water in danger of death by drowning. William Sinclair, brother to the devoted fawn, looks with fraternal regret at the vanishing bird and says: 'Indeed, my dear Jane, I never regretted my ignorance of swimming so much as I do this moment. The truth is, I cannot swim a stroke, otherwise I would save poor little Ariel for

154

your sake.' The father of the fawn, who was a minister, always at hand with spiritual consolation, says: 'Don't take it so much to heart, my dear child. Grief, girl, ought *not* to be so violent for the death of a favourite bird.'

Written as burlesque it would have been admirable. But for some reason, hidden deep in his own soul or in the circumstances of his life or the persuasions of his wife, Carleton did not intend it as burlesque. He was every bit as serious about the moral meaning of the character of Sir Thomas Gourlay, the central figure in the long boredom of the novel that was first called *Red Hall* and was later reprinted as *The Black Baronet*. His object in writing this novel was 'to exhibit in contrast, three of the most powerful passions that can agitate the human heart: love, ambition, and revenge.' Displaying the horror of the heart gripped by the claws of ambition Sir Thomas soliloquises in the style of tenth-rate tragedy: 'Well, well, I believe every man has an ambition for something. Mine is to see my daughter a countess, that she may trample with velvet slippers on the necks of those who would trample on hers if she were beneath them.' A harmless ambition, worthy of comic opera any day in the year, but a little more than ludicrous when placed in contrast with the gloom and villainy and clanking of chains in lunatic asylums with which Carleton surrounded it. Nor was it worthy of the comparison made by some literary friend who pointed out to Carleton that Massinger had treated a similar subject in *A New Way to Pay Old Debts;* nor was it really necessary for Carleton to state that when he wrote *Red Hall* he hadn't read a line of Massinger or even seen Sir Giles on the stage.

The stories of love-demented Jane and ambition-demented Sir Thomas may in their actual incidents have had some basis in fact. Of the latter he pointed out that 'the incidents seem to be extra-ordinary and startling but they are true'; and, although when writing *Jane Sinclair* he visited Grangegorman Asylum looking for copy and found 'to the honour of the sex' that no woman within those walls had gone mad for love, still the incidents in the fawn's tragedy are so insignificant that they might as well have happened as not have happened. He used the copy gathered then in Grangegorman when he coloured the story of the black baronet with interiors from a lunatic asylum, and in that curious way he linked up the black unreality of one novel with the white unreality of the other. For the incidents may have been based on fact, but the characters were unreal, their souls and the words in which they expressed their souls were unreal. Lucy Gourlay, the persecuted daughter of ambitious Sir Thomas, said to her lover: 'I know you may probably feel that this avowal ought to be expressed with more hesitation, veiled over by the hypocrisy of language, disguised by the hackneyed forms of mere sentiment, uttered like the assertion of a coquette, and degraded by that tampering with truth which makes the heart lie unto itself.' What Lucy meant to say was that she loved him, and being a man of great perseverance and penetration he eventually found it out. There were novels in which language like that was the vernacular. But it did not belong in the work of a man who had once seen the red-cheeked farmer's daughter smile at Denis O'Shaughnessy, heard her coaxing voice telling him to take the kiss and spare the King's English.

More unreal even than the sesquipedalianism that returned to him —not as a matter for mockery but as a medium of expression—in his lesser works and in his later days, was his moral purpose. A literary lady in present-day Ireland said somewhere, very foolishly, that Carleton had no moral purpose; a statement difficult to reconcile with any wide reading of Carleton's writings. If by 'moral purpose' is meant the intention to effect some general good by his writings then *Valentine McClutchy* and the tract about Art Maguire, the drunkard, and the skit about Paddy-Go-Easy and his wife, Nancy, are very definite evidence of effective moral purpose. They were effective even when offensive because they dealt with evident, practical things as tangible as the handle of a spade, something he could feel and judge with the cunning ability of the peasant. But beyond those tangible, visible realities, there was a world where moral purpose took his characters by the throat and deliberately strangled them. Something between moral purpose and malnutrition had set him prostituting his creative power for the benefit of Caesar Otway. Moral purpose brought forth Jane Sinclair and Sir Thomas Gourlay, one meant to be an angel and the other meant to be a monster, but both undeniably born dead. Moral purpose meant in the end that his genius dried up like water running into sand when in *The Double Prophecy* he sent Maria Brindsley to work diligently with her needle in a dressmaker's shop in Armagh City, her virtue fortified with whalebone stiff enough to resist the assaults of all the officers in the British army.

From this arid rigidity there was only one escape, only one gateway opening out into the green meadows, sending the man back along melodious, blossoming paths to find the boy who had died somewhere in the hard streets of Dublin, or in that hellhole of a cellar in Dirty Lane, or had been crushed to death by the burdens of life or the spectacle of the devastation of his people. Writing down the story of his youth he was doing naturally the thing that he did best of all: remembering and recording, until even the most trivial events became as full of moment as a major war, until the most insignificant people walked the sunlit earth with the stature and stride of demigods. He was at school again: in Jack Stuart's barn with Mrs. Dumont, and the thunders of revolution in France and Bonaparte's men on all the roads of Europe were echoes faint and far away; or in a hole in a clay-bank with Pat Frayne, at the death-bed of the tradition of Gaelic learning. Once again he was stealing Jack Stuart's apples, suffering from Jack Stuart's protective devices and becoming as a consequence the hero of all the boys of the neighbourhood. He was following the beautiful Anne Duffy from the place where Mass was said at the Forth, past Ned McKeown's crossroads where men argued about Bonaparte in two languages, down the hilly road to the village of Augher; and all the time the boy had, unknown to himself, been mapping out a path for the lazy, good-natured feet of Paddy-Go-Easy following Nancy from Mass and market. He was a candidate for the priesthood taking the long, hard road to Munster, torn one way by love of learning and another by love of home, until sleeping in a midland inn a bull roared in his dreams and decided the battle in his erratic soul.

Once again he was stretching his long legs along the road the pilgrims went to the holy island, not knowing then that one day he would find himself writing with a disapproving superiority of the people and forgetting the whole purpose of pilgrimage. Or he was trying his strength in Clogher Mill, or leaping the water at Clogher Karry, or watching the dancing of Buckramback, or hearing the fiddling of Mickey McRory, or turning the pages of Gil Blas and seeing a new world, coloured like the rainbow, opening out before him. His tragedy and the tragedy of his people was that the road he followed out of the valley did not lead to the end of the rainbow, did not lead him at all into a coloured land, but led instead past wayside gibbets and decaying bodies to the high stifling streets. There, appropriately enough, the best story that he had ever started to write ended abruptly.

Maybe that abrupt ending was the best thing that could have happened to that particular story. He had interesting things to tell about even in that latter portion of his life when all events were the writing of books and the reading of books, the meeting of people who read or wrote or published books. He could have written of his relations with Caesar Otway, although short of tearing his own soul into fragments it is doubtful if he could have made that business any clearer than it already was from external evidence. He could have given his final judgment of the men of Young Ireland, of Mangan alone of the men of that time comparable to him for tattered, wayward genius, of Duffy over the sea and Davis in an untimely grave, and John Mitchel shouting defiance of the British Empire in every land where he made his stay. He could have written of the future as he saw it in William Allingham, who sent to Carleton some of his

157

budding verses on the subject of frost and skating before daylight, and who hoped to see the verses published in the *Dublin University Magazine*. 'As to Poetry,' wrote Allingham, 'you ask me would I be content to herd with nameless creatures in an obscure corner of some periodical? I answer—certainly not.' Or he could have spoken of the passing time as it showed itself in John Banim who had written to him as to 'an honourable Irishman, as well as a fellow labourer in the unkindly soil of literature.'

He carried his story far enough to include his visit to Charles Robert Maturin, and he was possibly remembering that visit and his readings of Maturin's novels and stories when in later years he wrote the weird historical romance called *The Black Spectre* and sub-titled *The Evil Eye*. For that not very successful effort in the macabre was as near as Carleton ever got to the world of Mrs. Radcliffe. Maturin belonged to that world, not only because of the romance *Melmoth the Wanderer*, praised highly both by Scott and Byron, but by the eccentricities of his own existence, down to such a detail as the red wafer pasted on his brow when writing, to warn his family that he was creating and was not to be disturbed.[1] Carleton, fresh from the country, was admitted to the presence of this extraordinary creature in his house in York Street, found him dressed in a very slovenly manner, slippered feet, a loose cravat about his neck, a brown outside coat much too wide and too large, a tendency to become abstracted in the middle of a conversation, to raise an open hand and cry: 'Hush! I have an image.' The comment of the man who learned to be a writer but never forgot to be a sensible countryman was: 'After having left him, I would, had I possessed the experience which I do now, have pronounced him to be as vain a creature as ever lived.'

But there were other meetings that went unrecorded because the story ended when it did, other portraits in miniature that were never painted permanently for the benefit of times to come. There was his meeting in London with Thackeray whom he admired more than any other contemporary writer. (On his deathbed he re-read *The Newcomes*.) Thackeray, in his turn, had admiration for the *Traits and Stories*, thinking Carleton pre-eminent above all the novelists of the time in masterly knowledge of the human heart and in the expression of its emotions. To John McKibbin of Belfast Carleton delivered his opinions on Dickens and Thackeray, opinions possbly influenced by the memory of a pleasant meeting with one and something that looked not unlike avoidance of a meeting on the part of

[1] Maturin was the uncle of Oscar Wilde's mother; and Oscar Wilde, in his exile in France, called himself, after a Christian martyr and a Maturin book, Sebastian Melmoth.

the other: 'Thackeray is your great man in drawing the upper English. I spent an endeared day with him. He knows Ireland very well in an English way. He was pleased to tell me quite sincerely that in point of graphic delineation of life I was all their master. Dickens is fertile, varied, and most ingenious, but all is caricature. There does not appear a genuine, fine, sensible Englishman in all his works. His women are dolls and make-weights. The character of Pickwick is a compound of Uncle Toby and the Vicar of Wakefield.'[1]

In London he called also on Leigh Hunt and had apparently another endeared day. The only record of the visit that remains is in a letter written by Hunt some time later: 'I shall be most happy to see you, if you can come again. It will give me an opportunity of thanking you in person (strange motive to gratitude!) for having fairly torn me to pieces in sympathy with your poor miser Fardorougha—a thing which I had never contemplated as possible with a hater of miserliness, though I now see very well why it is quite so, and upon absolute brotherly grounds.'

To another friend Carleton once sent a copy of the *Nation* newspaper pointing out that it contained week after week what was 'probably the ablest and profoundest criticism of the day.' One critique to which he directed particular attention was written by a young lady, acquainted with all languages and all literatures, and all history, ancient and modern. Reasonably enough on that evidence he referred to her as 'the most extraordinary prodigy of a female that this country, or perhaps any other, has ever produced.' The young lady was to live to be a very good friend to Carleton, writing to him that a mind like his should not deliberately kill itself 'by conjuring up imaginary gloom.' His name, she said, was made; his reputation assured; he had a pension of two hundred pounds a year as well as a fine and clever family. He should go to Paris, chase gloom by a change of scene, take his daughters with him, make himself happy. 'God and the world have done more for you than for millions—one gave you genius, the other gave you fame; and if you want lessons of noble feelings, of lofty, elevated, pure, unworldly sentiment, go to your own books for them.' Only close friendship could sermon him in that accurate, incisive way without the certainty of permanent offence, and that woman lived on to talk tenderly of the novelist, William Carleton, to the poet, William Yeats. She signed her letter with the pen-name under which she found her place in the procession of Irish patriotic writers: 'Speranza'; and the woman who was to become the wife of William Wilde and the mother of Oscar Wilde certainly needed all the spirit that her name indicated.

[1] O'Donoghue, vol. ii.

There were so many places, so many people that his autobiography could have pictured had he, the story-teller, lived to write to the end the story of his own life. According to O'Donoghue he even neglected to include in the account of the early part of his life how he had written a letter in Latin to the commander of a British regiment asking admission into the ranks, and how the surprised officer had gently dissuaded him from hiding his classical talents under a red coat. The incident interestingly links him, the first novelist to write in English of the Irish people, with the randy story of one of the last great poets to write in Gaelic for the Irish people: with Red Owen O'Sullivan, Owen of the sweet mouth, the schoolmaster and spalpeen from the Kerry mountains, running from hunger and his own reputation and the mothers of his unlawful children into the army and navy of the English king. The man from Tyrone had, as far as we know, only hunger and poverty in pursuit, for his manly pride in being a lad with the girls had, apparently, nothing of the Munsterman's thoroughness. Another anecdote that he left unrecorded described how, searching for employment, he made his way into the shop of a bird-stuffer; and when the bird-stuffer, instinctively doubting the applicant's abilities, asked him how he stuffed birds, the reply—strong with all the sense of Ulster, Catholic and Protestant, Orange and Green—was that he stuffed birds with potatoes and meal.

The precedent of his omissions is as good an excuse as any for the use of selection and a mean in a study of the life that he lived. For he had himself the sense of the significance of the half-dozen great events in the life of every man. When he ended his autobiography he was describing how he had gone to teach school in the town of Carlow, bringing his young wife with him to poor lodgings that consisted of one small room about fourteen feet by ten. The coals supplied in the lodgings were 'of that vile and unhealthy description to be found in some of the coal-mines which lie between the counties of Carlow and Kilkenny.' The proportion of sulphur in the coals was very high and every morning the cream of sulphur lay so white and thick under the door that they could scrape it up with a knife. 'In fact the place was not habitable; not only we ourselves, but our children, became ill, and I found that to live there was only another word for death.'

That was the last sentence on the unfinished manuscript of the autobiography to which he had planned to devote his old age. With the pen poised in his hand he must have seen the ominous second meaning of those last nine words: 'to live there was only another word for death.' He had written down in great detail the golden record of the boyhood and youth that had made him, in much less detail the record of the early trials that had almost broken him.

There was still a great story to tell of meeting notable people and writing notable books, a great estimate to make of the past and present and future of Irish literature in relation to the Irish people. Those nine words may have warned him that his own story and the story of his people must return to horror, to the land in which to live was only another word for death.

For he was the story-teller talking of fun and coloured movement not in a contented house where all men were happy, but in a wake-house where all the noise and merriment was a mask or an antidote for mourning. Inevitably there would be at moments a lull in the fun, a break in the story, a silence with eyes turning to the door of the room where the body lay under-board, with waxen hands and face, and the brown shroud, and the soul gone out from suffering into unfathomable mystery.

His PORTRAIT, painted by J. J. Slattery, hangs in the National Gallery in Dublin in a room crowded with celebrities of his century. A very near neighbour is a dark gipsyish representation of Mrs. S. C. Hall, who was never drunk in the company of the Irish people. Slattery painted a long, strong, heavy face, hair going grey and thinning over the temples, a respectable black coat, a quill in the right hand, an elbow resting solidly on a copy of the *Traits and Stories of the Irish Peasantry*. It is, by all accounts, the best existing representation of the man, more alive with suggestion than the portrait by Charles Grey, more full of rough strength and the potentials of jumping energy than the strange photograph taken by Margaret Allen when Carleton was more than seventy, bearded like Tolstoy, gesturing with a hand no longer vigorous, his old eyes still oddly alive with imperishable humour.

His grave is in Mount Jerome cemetery on the south side of Dublin city. Standing there under dark cool chestnut trees I find it always difficult to realise that the body laid in the earth was old and feeble and heavily bearded. When the wind moves the long leaves and when a bird, venturing down into the city, sings suddenly from the branches, down in the earth the heart that responds must still be young and eager, and the body the strong body of the boy who idles forever in a green valley with the lost people of Ireland.

They buried him there in 1869 and some years later Jane Carleton was laid in the same clay. Below him in the city the people found new life and new leaders. Parnell rose and fell. The century came to an end with new writers and new ideas, and a new century came and revolution, and the city crept up the slope past him, smashing its way out through green hedges and grey walls towards the round blue mountains.

He was included in all that and half-forgotten in all that. A new nation grew up around him just as a growing city spread out and circled his grave. In all that growth he was praised and blamed, half-remembered and half-forgotten.

The present-day reader will find that O'Donoghue, in the first volume of the work often referred to, has catalogued the bulk of the published writings of William Carleton. From that list—or from the less complete list given in this book—the search for Carleton can go through libraries, second-hand bookshops, chimney corners, holes behind the hearth. Yeats, when, as a young man, he was writing from London to the United States the very valuable *Letters to the New Island,* complained of the scarcity of copies of the greater stories: *The Emigrants of Ahadarra; Fardorougha the Miser; Valentine McClutchy;* the *Traits and Stories.* To-day the position is, if anything, changed for the worse.

A century since a great Irishman said that the man who had not read William Carleton did not know the Irish people. The words are wisdom now as they were a hundred years ago. The approach to Carleton brings us to a period in the past when Irish faults and virtues were more strongly emphasised, more clearly distinguishable. This man saw deeply into the souls of his people, revealed in himself the torture of his time. He saw the sunshine on the valley and heard the birdsong as sun and song must have been in some ancient time. He heard his father tell stories and his mother sing songs as men and women in Ireland had told stories and sung songs for uncounted centuries. Then, with the figures that came from the mind of Le Sage dancing like imps down the road before him, he went on the world to find his fortune, saw the little roads lined with gallows, saw the black horror of famine. Around him in the ruin and within him in his own soul were the makings of modern Ireland.

Over his grave they raised in limestone a miniature obelisk. Miniature obelisks over graves were fashionable at that time. In limestone they carved on that obelisk a strong, bearded face. In limestone they wrote his name and ringed it in limestone with the poet's wreath of honour. And in limestone they wrote that the monument was erected by his widow and children: 'to mark the place wherein rest the remains of one whose memory needs neither graven stone nor sculptured marble to preserve it from oblivion.'